ON BEING A LIGHTING DESIGNER

Graham Walne

ENTERTAINMENT TECHNOLOGY PRESS

Application & Techniques Series

*I originally wanted to be a set designer back in the days when set designers also lit their own sets. Two things impacted on my future: one was the realisation that perhaps I wasn't cut out for set design and, two, the arrival at RADA where I was studying stage management, under Francis Reid.
He invited me to be his production electrician on many operas and slowly seduced me into lighting because he made it clear, straightforward, and fun. He later passed on many contacts in the opera world and watched my early days carefully.
Thank you Francis.*

Ruth Battle as The Salt Man in Spare Parts Puppet Theatre's production of 'The Farmer's Daughter' designed by Matt McVeigh and directed by Philip Mitchell. Photo: Simon Pynt.

ON BEING A LIGHTING DESIGNER

Graham Walne

Entertainment Technology Press

On Being a Lighting Designer

© Graham Walne

First published May 2019
Entertainment Technology Press Ltd
The Studio, High Green, Great Shelford, Cambridge CB22 5EG
Internet: www.etnow.com

ISBN 978 1 904031 94 9

A title within the
Entertainment Technology Press Application & Techniques Series
Series editor: John Offord

All rights reserved. No part of this publication may be reproduced in any material form (including photocopying or storing in any medium by electronic means and whether or not transiently or incidentally to some other use of this publication) without the written permission of the copyright holder except in accordance with the provisions of the Copyright, Designs and Patents Act 1988. Applications for the copyright holder's written permission to reproduce any part of this publication should be addressed to the publishers.

CODE / OBLD-001 05-19

CONTENTS

INTRODUCTION 11

1 YOU, THE DESIGNER 13
   Being a Lighting Designer 13
      What you can bring to the job: 14
      What training and education can bring to you: 14
   Why Should They Hire You? 14
   How Technical Do You Need to Be? 14
   Can You Make a Living From This? 15
   Are You Organised or Disorganised? 15
   Do You Like Working Alone? 16
   Make Sure Your Health Will Hold Out! 16
   Are You Dressed Correctly? 17
   What Do You Like Lighting? 18

2 YOUR WORKPLACE 19
   Will You Be There On Time? 19
   Managing Your Time Effectively 19
   Are You A Team Player? 19
   An Assistant 20
   Discrimination 20
   Speaking the Same Language 21
   Contracts 21
   Fees 22
   Who Owns What? 23
   Take Credit For Your Work 23

3 DESIGNING 25
   Design Language 25

Design Influences	27
Working with Set Designers	29
Have a Viewpoint	31
Discover The 'Wouldn't It Be Nice To's	32
Developing a Style	32
Is This Production True to Type?	34
Communicate!	34
A Benevolent Dictatorship?	35
Creative Development or Improvisation	35
Working on the Concept	36
Get Inside the Script but Don't Take it Too Literally	37
Let Your Lighting Tell a Story	38
Playing with Torches	38
Work Within or Challenging Limitations	39
Be Calculating in Unusual Locations	40
Power Choice	40
Moving Lights	41
Don't Take Lists for Granted	42
Don't Take Drawings for Granted!	43
Keep Lights Accessible	43
Redraw the Set Plan into Your System	43
Drawing Plans and Sections	44
Your Plan is Possibly the Best Yet!	46
How to Inspire a Lighting Designer	46

4   ON STAGE 51
    Do You Have Everyone's Contacts? 51
    Budgets and Schedules 51

Production Meetings 52
Be Green 52
Masking 52
   Who Does the Masking? 53
Should the Lights be Visible or Not? 54
Rehearsals 55
Safety, Insurance and Instructions 56
Involving the Crew 57
The Stage is Yours – Focusing 58
   Items which can slow the focus: 58
   Items which can speed the focus: 58
Operators – the Doorway to Your Design 59
Cheating 60
Assessing Lighting Changes 61
It's Not What We Had Before! 62
Breaks and Eye Strain 63
What Happens if You are Unwell? 63
What is a Lighting Design? 63

5 TIPS 67

Stage Etiquette 67
How Tidy is the Theatre? 67
Move About 67
Keep Some Up Your Sleeve 68
Costumes and Colour 68
Establish a File for Relights 69
Slowly But Surely, Gradual Improvements 69
Keep It Clean! 70
We Can Only Work at Night 70
It's All in the Music 72

Extra Ideas Need Extra Time – Effects	72
Projection	73
Sunrise and Sunsets	73
Painted Sets	73
Shadows	74
New Materials	75
Dealing with White Sets	76
Tipping the Mood One Way or the Other	78
Filling in the Holes!	78
One Person Shows	79
Laptop – Keep it Safe	79
Record the Hard Patch	79
Record The Heights of the Lighting Rig	80
Don't Be So Eager to Help	80
Prioritise Jobs List – Critical – Only You Can Tell – Cues	80
Running Cues Without Actors on Stage	80

6 REFLECTIONS 83

So What Did I Like Lighting?	83
Balancing the Logistics – The Bolshoi Ballet in a Concert Hall	84
Matching the Environment – Versailles	87
Less Successful	88
Is it Going to Get Any Better?	91
A Golden Memory – Anthony Newley	92
Did I Like All the Productions I Lit?	93

THE TEN COMMANDMENTS 95

ACKNOWLEDGEMENTS

The author has been given copies of all photographs used in this book on the understanding that the photographs are the property of the production company which has been credited. The lighting in all photographs is the copyright of the author. Should the photographer of any picture in this publication have a reasonable complaint that no suitable credit has been granted subsequent prints of this work can carry appropriate reference.

he electricians who have rigged, focused and operated my designs around the world all deserve a special thank you from me because without their interest in my design, their support and reliability, my task would have been considerably harder. When I worked in a new country for the first time - notably at Boston Opera and in Australia - the friendship of these people, some of which exists today across the decades and the oceans, brings back good memories. Thank you all.

10 On Being a Lighting Designer

INTRODUCTION

A lighting designer is a person who imagines what the lighting should look like on a production. They then develop that visualisation though the technology necessary to realise it and communicate that technology to the electricians who will rig the lighting before the lighting designer supervises the focus and the programming of the lighting control.

I have had the good fortune to have designed the lighting for over 500 productions on three continents over 50 years and this book details the approach I have learned and employed; it can be read as a sequence of tasks or as a work of reference.

This book is hardly the first on stage lighting: that honour probably goes to "Manual for Constructing Scenes and Machines in the Theatre" written in 1638 by Nicola Sabbatini (and which also described stage mechanics) and detailed how banks of stage lights should be positioned and operated at the same time. The Italians had developed lights with reflectors, light sources and lenses which contained water coloured to change their effects and drawings of this equipment closely resembled what we use today.

The history of drama also tells us that the use of light was a key factor in theatres even before Sabbatini. Shakespeare's Macbeth, thought to have been first performed in 1606, was performed at the indoor theatre at Blackfriars in London where the darkness and candle light was thought to have been carefully used to evoke atmosphere.

Limelight was discovered in the 1820s when its intensity made it useful in surveying and, by 1836, the powerful device had become a valuable stage light; it was first used in the Opera House (later Royal Opera House) at Covent Garden in 1837 and over the following years its use spread rapidly. Its ability to highlight performers made it the first followspot.

Report of great actors (such as Sir Henry Irving, the first actor to be knighted) praised their charismatic abilities but, it is also likely that the actors knew that they had to stay close to the centre of the stage where the limelights could easily focus on them and they were the brightest thing on stage!

We tend to think of lighting as a modern art but it is clear that for centuries people have experimented with light to enhance their performances and engage their audiences.

Possibly the first use of light for a performance outside a theatre building was a son-et-lumiere at Château de Chambord in France in 1952. Today, stage lighting is used in events, displays, promotions, military tattoos, outdoor concerts and openings and the people responsible can have successful careers in these venues without ever setting foot in a theatre.

If the use of light goes back centuries then the term 'design' goes back even further to Latin and then onwards to other early European languages. Etymological dictionaries indicate the term originally meant 'devise', 'mark out', 'draw' and 'plan', all words which we would use today to describe what designers do. In the past the lighting was "done" by the electrician or the producer and the term lighting designer might not have been used; lighting people weren't originally recognised in the credits or on the playbills.

The idea of an individual responsible for the lighting and recognised first for their imagination before their technical knowledge is comparatively recent, nevertheless, today's lighting designers would recognise the creativity of their earlier counterparts.

From these early days the work of what we now call a lighting designer embraces realising visual images and reproducing them through carefully chosen equipment, positions and colours, before balancing combinations and intensities of the lights in time with specific actions or emotions on stage.

Lighting design puts productions on a higher plane of enjoyment and understanding and over the past decades as the profession has developed, lighting design has become a key component of milestone productions worldwide and, has stimulated and supported development in related art techniques such and set and projection design – it has also encouraged improvements to lighting equipment. Today lighting designer bodies such as the UK's Association of Lighting Designers[1] is sufficiently recognised internationally that it is working with the European Union to monitor the effects of legislation on lighting equipment criteria.

When lighting designers start work on stage things start to happen. The set is assembled, masking put in place and working lights are switched off, a single unfocused spotlight pierces the darkness and the magic begins. Lighting designers are good to have around!

---

1 Association of Lighting Designers. PO Box 955, Southsea, PO1 9NF UK Telephone: 07817 060189 . https://www.ald.org.uk.

1 YOU, THE DESIGNER

Being a Lighting Designer

Whilst this book is less about the equipment than the process, there is, nevertheless, a significant piece of 'equipment' without which no lighting design would be possible, namely the lighting designer! I suggest, therefore, that some words about keeping this piece of equipment both in good working order and, in the most appropriate frame of mind, might be helpful.

Some years ago whilst lighting at the University of West Virginia I was interviewed by the local media in front of my crew. It was the first time any of us had met. "What do you first look for in your crew?" I was asked, and without considering the answer carefully I replied: "A sense of humour." This simple answer nevertheless carries much accuracy because with humour stress can be diffused, relationships preserved and problems solved.

There is always a dilemma for young lighting designers (especially in the early years when contacts are few) torn between the regular employment offered by a resident company and the freer but riskier environment of being freelance.

There is much to be learned when as a resident staff member, one is lighting several productions in the same venue because the same equipment, positions and techniques can be tested against earlier ideas in the same venue and thus analysed in a way which is not as easy when working as a freelance with different companies in different venues.

Part of this process relates to one's job description. Many excellent lighting designs are produced by resident head electricians, some of whom do not think of themselves as designers (and yet they are making aesthetic choices) but prefer the stability of a regular income.

Lighting designers also work alone for much of the time and work with crew for shorter periods then would be the case with, say, set and costume designers. Thus it is helpful if one is content with one's own company and does not always require having other people around.

What you can bring to the job:
- a sense of humour;
- a perspective about the role of the arts in today's world;
- natural good health (more important than fitness);
- a preparedness to accept the lifestyle changes.

What training and education can bring to you:
- an environment in which your creativity can be nurtured;
- a broadening of your general knowledge and skill;
- a professional attitude to drugs, timekeeping, attitude and dress;
- competence, skill and knowledge in your chosen career.

Why Should They Hire You?

The short answer is presumably because they like the style of lighting that you do. But there are other complementary reasons too.

These include:
- How well you work with others
- How you solve the director's problems
- How you stick to the schedule and the budget
- How much is your fee!

Put simply, if you throw tantrums and go over budget you'd better deliver something extraordinary to compensate but I wouldn't suggest you adopt this as a strategy; there are a lot of hungry lighting designers out there!

So, be clear about what you can offer and work on those aspects of what you do which aren't as strong. To be really successful you need to have a sense of the contribution you can make and its part in the destiny of your client.

How Technical Do You Need to Be?

Historically most lighting designers emerged from the ranks of electricians who were asked to provide lighting for events. Consequently they had a technical background which helped them to interpret their creative ideas to the team that would rig, focus and plot their ideas.

Today the technology is much more complicated than it was only a couple of decades ago so designers do need to know (for example) about the complexities of different types of colour mixing and how different control systems can deliver effects. The early decisions about the choice of equipment will inevitably also involve analysis of technical data (and cost) but the arbiters should always be creative.

In this it is critical that you stay up to date with developments in production styles, equipment and regulations. This means subscribing to as many regular publications as you can, attend trade shows, become a member of trade associations or professional bodies and just keep taking note of others' work.

Can You Make a Living From This?

When young designers start out, maybe fresh from college, it is usual that the opportunity to work is more important than the fee.

To an extent companies do trade on this but then they are providing opportunities in return. New, young companies are also exciting places to work because of their energy and willingness to challenge the establishment.

It used to be very difficult for a young designer to know what fee to charge and I know several producers who were embarrassed at the negotiations. But then professional bodies and trade unions (notably in the USA and the UK) established minimum fees for designers for all types of work (including related expenses) and these were an enormous help.

Production companies generally have a base fee which is calculated from the budget for the show and these usually stay much the same for the same type of show.

I keep a record of the hours I spend on a production so that I can then amortise the fee across the hours and see what hourly rate I've been working for. Interestingly this is also useful to feed back into schedules to inform how long you might typically need to draw the plan and how long you need to focus and so on.

Are You Organised or Disorganised?

Much of lighting design is about managing data, the details of the venue, the equipment, the schedule, the budget, your colleagues, your transport and your accommodation. If you are not naturally efficient then these elements will manage you and your lighting will suffer. Fortunately, today there are numerous items of software which can help. These include spreadsheets for budgets, project management software for schedules and lighting design software which can provide an inventory of the rig and even calculate the rental cost. Of course, you have to collate your data first before you can use any of these systems to some degree, remember Garbage In Garbage Out!

Do You Like Working Alone?

When you start employment you may not have had any experience of working with others, you may not know if you like being part of a team or prefer being left alone to do a job. For much of the time a lighting designer is alone, for example, when travelling, staying in hotels, working on the plan and the design. Conversely, when in the theatre the lighting designer works with others as part of a team, but, no-one else in that team shares responsibility for the lighting design.

This is a complex working arrangement because, for example, the lighting design relies heavily on the lighting crew and the lighting designer can instruct them but is not responsible for them, is not their line manager. In this respect, when in the theatre the lighting designer can be surrounded by people but is ultimately making decisions alone about the lighting. Not everyone adapts well to this structure and especially in the early years it is useful to monitor how you are reacting to the different pressures so that you can manage them.

Make Sure Your Health Will Hold Out!

The theatre is an arduous profession because it can expose people to stress, irregular mealtimes, unhealthy food, and loss of sleep. There might also be physical and environmental pressures too, extremes of temperature for example, and physical hazards. However, lighting designers are not as exposed to these risks for as long as some other members of the production team but, nevertheless, it is critical to understand what your body needs, and what it doesn't if you are to survive.

Firstly, it is useful to know if you are naturally at your best in the morning or at night because the safety and quality of your work will be better if it can be scheduled accordingly; related to this is also a sense of how much sleep you require and how your body needs and processes foods of different types.

No kind of drugs should be tolerated, especially for those exposed to risks and operating stage machinery.

When equipping yourself for the task in hand it is also important to assess the effects that the temperature of the environment will have on you during the long day in the theatre.

Sometimes the heating is turned down or even off to save money. This happened to me when lighting the Bolshoi Ballet in the USA and in temperatures of 40° F, so the crew and I equipped ourselves with thermal underwear – not especially sexy – but most certainly effective!

Here in Australia, where this book is being written, late spring and early autumn can see considerable changes in temperature and a tee shirt and shorts which might be de-rigeur at noon would be inadequate at night. These considerations can become important if people are away from home, or their hotel, for very long periods.

My comments above about sleep, diet and clothing might seem trifling, especially to a younger generation, but lighting requires all your concentration and it is wise to remove distractions.

Are You Dressed Correctly?

This may seem an odd question but how you are dressed can influence how others judge you at first and whether you are comfortable during the day.

For example, when I lit the Bolshoi Ballet in London the company's senior executives and set designers all wore suits and ties and I was out of place in my casual gear. I didn't speak Russian so there was already a gap to bridge. Once I started wearing a suit the executives become more cordial and this was the key to negotiating.

Of course I had to balance this against how the suit made me appear to my crew but I found they understood simply because I had to spend a lot of time with the executives and they felt it "went with the territory".

Comfort is a key factor in removing distractions so that you can concentrate fully on lighting. It is not only what you wear that matters but how often and how close by you have access to food and water. The management should schedule breaks for these but often such breaks are eroded by events.

What Do You Like Lighting?

Unless you are very lucky as a young designer and become associated with a specific company it is more usual to accept a range of work simply to pay the bills. In time you can specialise, concentrating on particular companies, particular scales of work and, particular types of work.

It would be inaccurate for older designers to claim that they have enjoyed every production they have worked on, certainly I cannot. However, I can claim to have enjoyed *playing with light.*

Over the years I have been lucky to light almost every type of work, primarily drama, dance, opera and pantomime but I would not say I was known for any specific type of work.

2 YOUR WORKPLACE

Will You Be There On Time?

People coming into the theatre industry for the first time (perhaps like any job) are often surprised at the importance given to punctuality. I grew up in stricter times; as a student at RADA (the Royal Academy of Dramatic Art) three late marks meant you were considered for expulsion and later at the London Palladium premium variety theatre similar strictures were applied. I am naturally punctual but I have worked with people who aren't. If this is you then this means you need to employ systems in your life to overcome these bad habits. For example:

- Prepare your clothes, files and tools the night before
- Set two alarms in different systems in case one fails
- Work out how long it takes to get to a new destination
- Set off earlier in case there are unavoidable delays
- If you're early go for a coffee
- And don't be irritated if others are later than you!

Time is money and money is always tight in theatre.

Managing Your Time Effectively

It's wise to develop a sense of how long it takes you to do the various tasks concerned with realising a lighting design, not only those tasks in the theatre itself but the others concerned with getting out of the house and also at working at your desk.

You don't need to, and shouldn't become obsessive about this but the ability to plan your day effectively could just mean more time to refine a focus, more time to revisit a cue and more time just to sit in the stalls and absorb what is happening on stage.

Are You A Team Player?

I was once talking with a professor of industrial psychology at a theatre trade fair in the UK. He made an interesting observation that theatre was rare as an industry in that people, often previously unknown to each other, are brought together to undertake complex tasks as a team but without much explanation of what is involved, the team members know their jobs and how their work fits with that of others. (I suspect there are actually several occupations of which this is accurate, such as paramedics and pilots, but it is certainly true of theatre).

Good teamwork means achieving a creative balance between your personal taste and experience and those of your colleagues. However, the balance can be tilted in favour of those with higher status! Some directors and producers prefer to use much the same team for each production knowing that their familiarity with each other's methods should result in a more peaceful (and often more economic) environment.

An Assistant

Over a lifetime in lighting I have only had an assistant a few times and always because the person has been supplied automatically by the company, never because I asked for an assistant. With hindsight this omission might not have been wise. Where I have had an assistant I have learned that they can share the load of the rigging check, the focusing and help share the load of refocusing and re-plotting as it arises.

Sometimes assistants can take over on late overnight calls so the lighting designer can get some sleep, fresh for the following day (but this can be expensive!). Sometimes assistants are specialists in specific areas to supplement the lighting designer's own skills. For example, they might concentrate on projection or moving light programming. Being an assistant to an established lighting designer is also a good way of learning and making connections.

Discrimination

This book is being written during a period of considerable media attention across the world on the behaviour of notable people in film, stage and television. Against this background I feel I should offer budding theatre lighting designers a few observations. I have been lucky enough to light a lot of productions on three continents and I am not aware of any discrimination or improper behaviour on any of them.

It is wise to note here that lighting designers are high profile people working with all layers of a production from producers, stars, crew to cleaners and drivers. These interactions take place frequently when people are under stress and how you behave in these circumstances can affect not only your future but also that of others.

Speaking the Same Language

As I have mentioned, when I lit the Bolshoi Ballet my task was complicated by my inability to speak Russian so a translator was provided both for the UK season and for my visits to Moscow. Over time I discovered that the nationality of the translator made a difference to how the translations went, and consequently to any negotiations.

Some of the translators were world-class, but some Russians feared of communicating any of my explanations to their Russian masters in case I wasn't agreeing with them and the plotting became tense. On the other hand English translators seemed to me to communicate without editing and this enabled the Russian director to understand better what the problems were and help overcome them.

Contracts

There is nothing to stop you writing your own contract, as an expression of what conditions you require of those engaging you to light the production. However, the producer might not be prepared to work to a document of your own drafting and might prefer to use a contract created by a national or international body. These standard lighting designer contracts are comprehensive and cover the following items:

- Copyright
- Billing
- Further Use of Lighting Design
- Archive Material
- Budget
- Staffing Approval
- Equity Bond
- Accommodation
- Transportation
- Per Diems
- Miscellaneous Expenses

- Tickets
- Office Spaces and Access
- Information
- Design Disclaimer
- Insurance
- Indemnification

(There is another excellent reason to connect with the lighting designer bodies mentioned above. As this book is being written regulations produced by the European Union threaten to change the kind of light sources and equipment we use in the performing arts.

The UK Association of Lighting Designers in particular has done outstanding work studying the proposed regulations and seeking to put their impact into a context which will not harm our industry.)

Fees

Lighting Designers have traditionally lagged behind their earlier counterparts in set design with regard to the size of their fees.

More recent specialisms of sound and media perhaps are in a similar position today but, over the last three decades it has become commonplace for designers of all types to receive a percentage of the gross box office income as a royalty, typically 1%. This can help to boost income and on successful productions, such as Broadway and West End musicals, this has made some designers very wealthy.

I have worked with some producers who preferred to negotiate low fees on the basis that if royalties were agreed as an addition the producers could deflect that these did not come out of the main budget (they come out of the box office income)!

One producer I worked for over several years specialised in productions touring around the UK. The producer noticed that I always stayed in the best hotels wherever I was working and made the assumption that my fees could be lower if only I didn't have an apparently extravagant lifestyle! Whilst there is a logic to this statement I explained how my fees were calculated (on the basis of time allocated) and further that for me at least, the pressure of an 18-hour day, at the end of which I had to deliver a show, was alleviated by being able to sink into a hot bath with a glass of wine and enjoy room service. In fact, once the producer understood the fee basis it was increased to cater for additional services I hadn't known would be required!

In Boston, USA I lit 25 major operas over five years, commuting across the Atlantic from London every three weeks during the season. Eventually I became the company's highest paid designer but this was predicated on two facts. The first was that being out of the UK and away from my office for weeks at a time (and before email) my other work stopped and consequently I wasn't earning from those sources.

The second was that my style used less equipment than my predecessors (all distinguished, talented and beloved designers in their own right) and since all the equipment was rented the company saved money overall even after my fee, airfares and hotel bills were taken into account.

Who Owns What?

In most countries the theatre world has access to contracts for services and where there are trade unions then often the contracts are not generic but highly specialised and tailored to particular skills, lighting being one example.

Occasionally lighting designers have to share a rig with another lighting designer. This often happens when two productions are in repertoire say in a large opera or ballet theatre or perhaps during a festival. Both these instances have happened to me and both occasions went smoothly. But it raises the question of who owns what part of the design and is this reflected in the contract? This will be explored later.

Take Credit For Your Work

Lighting designers have historically had to fight for recognition of their work especially on such items as posters and in programmes. To some extent this is because chief (or master) electricians and the director (previously called the producer) were often responsible for the lighting and a separate dedicated person for the lighting was very rare. Eventually lighting designers made such a difference, and moved beyond simple illumination, that their contribution was seen as positive and worthy of note.

24 On Being a Lighting Designer

3 DESIGNING

Design Language

Until recently and, amongst the team of people who create a production, the lighting designer lacked easy access to ways of demonstrating what the end result might be. The set designer can produce models and drawings, the costume designer can display materials and sketches, the sound designer can play recordings of effects and music. Writers can read excerpts from the script, composers can play musical numbers, dancers can try new moves.

In the past however, the lighting designer could not easily produce in the office or rehearsal room a three dimensional image in light, shade and colour (although many successful lighting designers obtained their early work though the mesmeric effects of a model theatre).

This problem of communicating visual ideas verbally has often led to some lack of alignment about the picture on stage between the director and the lighting designer when the lighting is being balanced and plotted.

This is because the words which members of the creative team tend to use also tend to lack precise definitions – 'magical', 'dramatic', 'lyrical', 'stark' and 'colourful'. Directors also use more precise words to describe the desired 'look' of the production – here are some which have been used in my conversations with directors:

Classicism – a form of work which follows established rules.

Romanticism – this term, which relates to a literary and artistic movement in the late 18th Century, is used to describe work which can be subjective, passionate, perhaps inappropriate and, by contrast to classicism, which follows no rules.

Expressionism – this term, which relates to an art movement in the early part of the 20th Century, is used to describe the use of exaggeration, distortion, strong colours, simplified shapes and lines to convey emotion rather than naturalism.

Stylistic – this term is used to describe work produced in the manner of a particular period, artist or movement.

Film Noire – a term used to describe usually dramatic black-and-white films of the 1940s and 1950s in which the lighting comprised very specific highlights, often on parts of the face or body, contrasted with bold shadows.

All the above can be interpreted subjectively so that each person might think they understand what is being said, and might have an image in their head, but is it the same image? In all the above cases it is very helpful to be able to share a common point of reference such as a painting or a recent film. However, the recent use of CAD programs offers some ability to render an image of a set in terms of the effect upon it of light, shade, direction and colour and this is helping to overcome miscommunication. Often the CAD program will also provide the ability to plot the lights into a laptop which can then carry the initial ideas to the theatre's own lighting desk and save time in plotting again.

The nature of theatre has changed over the years and reflecting industry in general its decision-making structure has moved from the pyramidal and hierarchical to the flatter. The distribution of skills within the industry has also changed. 50 years (and more) ago, in the absence of lighting designers, directors frequently lit their own productions and set designers were frequently lighting designers too.

Some directors I have worked with have told me the technology today is too complex for them to stay abreast of it enough to light their own shows and direct as well. Whilst this is perhaps understandable nevertheless design is concerned with images and the technology is merely in place to realise the imagery. Some directors with whom I have worked have referred to films or paintings as a way of communicating how the production should look, for example, one opera director said to me "I want it very Rembrandt!"

Thus a director could still make design statements if someone else interprets them technically. In lighting it is still true that the lighting designer has to communicate his or her design to the rigging crew by means of scale drawing of the lighting rig itself, precisely annotated with the circuitry, colouring and nature of the instruments. Few other areas of design are required to deliver this level of communication. For example, whilst most set designers can produce working drawings, it is also true that most scene shops take considerable data from the model. Costume shops too don't require the designer to produce patterns but a sketch and material samples; they will do the rest once the actor is in place.

The older method of developing the stage picture tended to involve only the director and set designer, frequently locked away for weeks before anyone else saw the first stages of the model. These early visual discussions seldom involved the lighting designer. Often there was a tendency to this because the lighting was 'done' last and so people assumed it needn't be thought about till last. I have certainly been banned from the rehearsal room because the director wasn't ready to talk about lighting! I think the development in lighting over more recent decades has moved the art of lighting from being passive illumination to an active participation in the experience of the production.

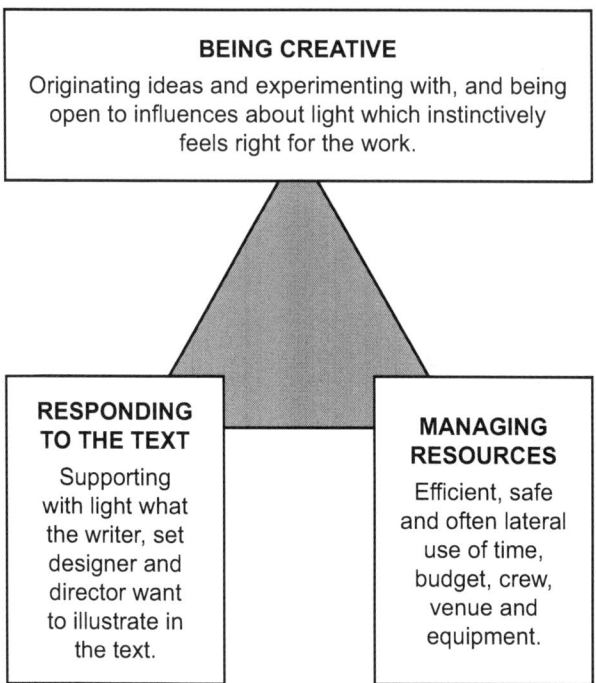

For me a good lighting design is one which achieves a balance between these elements.

Design Influences

In the classical repertoire Greek and Shakespearean work was originally produced in venues with little or no scenery. The later physical developments in building did enable larger theatres, and therefore larger stages, to be constructed.

The Victorians in the UK relished spectacle and much of the effects we marvel at today are simply updated and electrified versions of manually or clockwork powered machines originally designed over 150 years ago.

But what great writing emerges from this period? Is it true that the growth of scenery and spectacle coincides with a decline in the creation of work we still cherish? If this is true what of later building cycles in Edwardian times and the 1960s?

An examination of the locations of drama plots over the years also reveals that today the landscape changes with filmic or televisual rapidity whereas decades ago one location (and therefore one set) was all that was needed either all evening or at least until the interval.

Today's minimalism relates both to the need to make quick changes of scene but also to the need to respect tighter budgets. Although it is hard to say if theatre has always been impoverished, certainly it has always needed its benefactors, such as powerful nobility in Shakespeare's day, multinational companies or state agencies today.

Did all these influences, cost-effectiveness, film and television bring about a move away from realism at some point? Stage can never compete with film and television for realism, even if some of that is ironically produced digitally rather than in actual form. Noted UK designer Timothy O'Brien says: "Cinema has taught [designers] that a story may be told through hints and startling juxtapositions."

Britain's long standing love affair with its language, at least with those who used it well, Shakespeare, Dickens, Milton and, more recently, including Robert Bolt, has perhaps bred a suspicion of theatre forms and production wherein the spectacle swamps the words.

One of the most financially and artistically successful new theatres to have been built in the UK in recent years is Sam Wanamaker's reconstruction of Shakespeare's Globe, dedicated to the word and adding or needing, little else. I have the honour of having been a small part of its design team.

Recent years have seen more cross fertilisation between the art forms as theatre directors move into opera and then on into film and then back again to the theatre.

Scenery is no longer a Restoration-style background providing a suitable location against which the story or the action unfolds. Today the scenery (and consequently the costumes, sound and lighting too) has become a major character.

Herein lies the key to the success of the design. It is vital that this additional character, additional in the sense that it wasn't created by author or composer, is appropriate to the piece. Both designers and directors have favourite techniques and styles and will be influenced by their need to follow or contradict current fashion. Often these forces act upon a production to its disadvantage, setting the mind off on an interesting and visually stimulating direction but one which has little relevance to the piece (and one which often requires unusual amounts of gymnastics from the performers).

Such indulgence breeds the temptation to deliberately set a piece in untypical and radical surroundings, out of period or location, so that press attention will at least record the director or designer's names if not a slight increase in curious box office. Perhaps Shakespeare's work has 'suffered' this way more than any other playwright, but equally quality work will survive long after the contortions have been forgotten.

Setting a piece outside its natural home and period is a balance of what is relevant and what is no longer practised. 'History repeats itself' remains a truism and thus any piece concerned with human behaviour is likely to remain relevant, but if the manners and mores of the piece are not as contemporary as the costumes and props then these may seem out-of-place and distracting.

The impact, potential and actual, which the set has to move the audience cannot be underestimated.

Set, costume and lighting all have the ability to make an instant statement in a way which a single word cannot. Our eyes receive information instantly and we react to it; the words take a little longer and we need to have several of them before we can understand where the sentence is going.

Of course both the visual and the aural picture could be tricks; they might then change into something rather different.

Working with Set Designers

I have been lucky to enjoy good relationships with many set designers and I have found good set designers (engaged well before lighting designers) introduce you to their designs with an air of mystery because their set is telling a story and seduces you into it revealing its secrets; then you're hooked and you just have to see how it behaves when it's lit. One wonderful designer I've worked with often in Australia, Zoe Atkinson, works like this and on the first night of one extremely complex production Zoe said to me: "I'll never get to Heaven." "Why?" I asked. she replied: "Because when I get to the Pearly Gates, St Peter will say you can't come in – you've been terribly cruel to lighting designers!"

Simon Ash's design for the London premiere of 'Winnie The Pooh' was inspired by the Shepard drawings and in introducing me to the model he said: "You won't get any side lighting in because there are two big flats up and downstage, you won't be able to put the ladders on stage because the sloping floor is covered in gorse bushes, oh and you won't be able to have the bars too low because there are two tall trees that go round on the revolve – there's also a front gauze in some scenes – yes – I think I've thought of everything!" Now I like a challenge and this was certainly one; it was resolved by under-slinging short lighting bars in the gaps between the trees and lowering them to the stage where the focus could be estimated before raising them to check and then repeat the process for adjustment.

Simon Ash's setting (inspired by E.H. Shepard's drawings) for the world premiere (1990) of Vanessa Ford's Production of Glyn Robbin's play based on Winnie the Pooh, directed by Richard Williams. London Royalty Theatre. Photo Lynton Black.

Simon's banter belied the close working relationship we had and underneath it we shared a desire to deliver the essence of AA Milne's work. I think there is a clue there to working with others; you are serving a common admiration of the work above any other partisan issues.

Sometimes set designers are legendary. When I was a kid I spent a lot of time looking through books of set designs and one I especially remember by a Chinese American designer called Ming Cho Lee. Imagine how I felt when, years later, Ming designed the set for a production of 'Turandot' for Boston Opera and I was to meet him. Despite the fact that he had never heard of me he was instantly warm and cordial, professional and inspiring as he made adjustments to his design (See illustration under "How to Inspire a Lighting Designer" on page 46).

Another legend was Valeri Levethal who, when I first met him was the senior designer in the (then) Soviet Union and who I worked with in the US, the UK and in Moscow. Valeri was a small pixie-like figure with twinkling eyes and a passion for his scenery. He came from a culture that didn't have lighting designers in the western sense; the lighting in Valeri's day was processed by a specially chosen electrician working to the set designer's instructions. I respected this approach with Valeri and he respected my design ability. From him I adopted once of his favourite phrases, referring to the gentle use of light "just touch it".

I noticed with Ming and Valeri, but by no means restricted to them, the sense of ownership they had for their sets – more perhaps a sense of family. I watched Valeri once in Edinburgh as the massive Bolshoi sets were reduced to fit the smaller stage – "My poor scenery" he lamented.

Have a Viewpoint

I suggest that most of the notable artists, writers and musicians in history have created works around a philosophy or around a specific viewpoint. For example, Dickens' writing illustrated the poverty and abuses of the time, the French Impressionists wanted to paint light, much of Wagner's approach to music, drama and staging influenced later opera. I'm not suggesting that lighting designers need to espouse significant causes but if you can find an aim or theme to your work it will make it easier for clients to identify and use you because they want their production to benefit from that aim or that theme.

Discover The 'Wouldn't It Be Nice To's

Directors have become more confident today than they used to be about talking with lighting designers. I think this is partially because there is greater understanding that lighting design is firstly about light not about equipment. In past decades I found some directors nervously made lighting suggestions prefaced with "wouldn't it be nice to ..." This was a signal that what followed was what they really wanted to see but were reluctant to ask for outright. I think those days have gone but it still follows that to everyone in the creative team there is usually something they feel enhances their work and or the narrative. Listen out for these, there's a chance some other members of the creative team have been on the production longer than you and might know more about it. Try and incorporate these hints into your design, they might just work and, your colleagues might remember your help next time.

Developing a Style

All designers develop a style which identifies their work and clients hire designers because they want that style used in their commission. In lighting, styles are often shaped by the nature of the work itself.

Modern dance, for example, is very different from classical dance, utilising more lighting changes, more colour and angle changes. So, if a designer were to specialise in one of these above the other his or her lighting style will reflect the characteristics of the work itself.

It's inevitable that you will be drawn to particular lighting angles and positions because you feel it looks good for the production. For example, I like crosslight, usually from the sides in the wings. I like the crispness this gives to the outline on the performers and the potential to isolate them if required. However there are a number of factors which need to be in place for this approach to work and the consequences of them. Firstly, crosslight if not supplemented by light from other angles produces a dark line down the centre of the face and body and this is not always appropriate, it can be too dramatic. Therefore a front light, or fill, at right angles to the side light can be touched in to soften the dark line. This approach requires open wings in which the masking, usually but not always black, is on and offstage. Lighting units are concealed by the wings and the stray light passes through the gaps and offstage.

There are pluses and minuses with repeating what you have done before. The same things might save time but it might also be boring and if applied without thinking it might be inappropriate. Trying new colours, equipment and angles might take longer but it also might discover something otherwise unconsidered and hidden.

But sometimes the set design does not provide for open wings and therefore it is possible to put the side light higher on the ends of the lighting bars (known as an 'end pipe' shot in the USA, or 'high sides'), here the light beam passes over the sides of the set into the acting area. This position retains the crispness but puts light on the floor where bounce or reflected light might be obtrusive and so the intensity and colour of the high side light needs care.

If there are no wings in which to mask the lighting units then the impact of these elements on the style of the production needs to be discussed with the director and set designer. I've recently lit a production in which the backstage elements were visible because they provided an industrial feel. Some of the lenses needed masking by barndoors or black foil because they were too distracting.

So my approach relies heavily on the ability to use crosslight or high sides and producers who use me a lot know that is my style.

William McInnes & Khan Chittenden in "Equus" – Perth Theatre Company's production at His Majesty's Theatre Perth Western Australia (2009). Directed by Melissa Cantwell. Photo: Ashley de Prazer.

Is This Production True to Type?

It's very tempting immediately after receiving a commission to start dreaming how you might approach the design; maybe the work is already known to you if it is a revival, and/or the venue and other members of the creative team are known to you so you think you already have something to start with. It's tempting to make assumptions on these bases. But the simple reality is that until you meet the creative team and are introduced to the work any ideas are guesses. For example, a colleague of mine was once asked to light a London production of 'Macbeth'; he had seen some productions elsewhere and had also researched how the play was mounted originally so he had lots of ideas for dark backgrounds and shafts of light. The director however wanted a modern production lit with fluorescent light!

Communicate!

Many years ago I lit an opera in a small private theatre. The opera had been composed by its director and conductor (who also owned the theatre).

Given that the work was untried it seemed reasonable to me that the director never spoke to me during the first rehearsals; he was, after all, extremely busy. As this went on I began to wonder if my lighting was doing what he wanted and I sought an opportunity to ask.

He reassured me that one benefit of hiring me was that he didn't have to worry about the lighting and he could devote precious time to other aspects. This was naturally very reassuring but I think both of us learned a lesson – talk to each other!

Another good example of this occurred when I was on the staff of the Royal Academy of Art in London. The head of training, Dot Tenham, and a revered person to all who passed through her hands, ruled that, unless production staff were actually working a performance they would turn up in her office twice daily for morning coffee and afternoon tea.

Some busy crew resented this but, sitting casually with cup in hand many technical issues were gently resolved. Wise lady. Good and relaxed communications are essential.

As the production comes together several aspects might not work as it was anticipated they would (including actor's performances). Some of these aspects can be changed but as time and money run out radical changes are unlikely. Enter the lighting designer who can, at the touch of a switch, conceal parts of the stage and make others change shape and colour. This does not mean that the lighting designer is more powerful than other members of the creative team but it does mean that the director may well ask for effects which at first appear to the lighting designer to be at odds which what was discussed in the early days. It's just possible the director has a lot on his or her mind and lacks the time to explain more fully, just go with the flow and see what happens! As long as what you had plotted is stored on the lighting desk you can experiment without fear.

In some situations members of the creative team can offer ideas to other members. This certainly occurs during early rehearsals, improvisation and creative development. It can be stressful if the ideas are simply not practical but maybe, just maybe, there is the kernel of something in the suggestion that is worth exploring.

If this situation is undisciplined it can create more distractions than direction. I was once lighting in Boston when the company's legendary sound designer Gary Harris (a person then in opera not mentioned or credited and hidden behind a screen) mentioned he could, from his vantage point, see some lights which had been knocked which, from the centre stalls production desk I could not. After thanking him Gary then explained that on Broadway one discipline is simply not allowed to discuss another's work. Too much communication is perhaps as bad as too little!

A Benevolent Dictatorship?

The workings of the creative team that put together productions are interesting in how they have reflected the changes in our broader society. When I started lighting 50 years ago now, the structure was more vertical than it is today and the producer (who provided the money) was close to the director who guided the creative decision making. Today the structure is flatter and it allows the creative members a greater say although the producer and director still have the final word.

Creative Development or Improvisation

The genesis and delivery of most productions are usually based on a chronological sequence. A single person might first have the idea for the work and then develop that into a written (visual or musical) concept.

After this the concept is usually progressed with a director under the producer's aegis. After this it is not usual for all members of the creative team to be involved at the same time. Here I am making a distinction between those who help to create the work and those who then help to realise it. Typically the set designer would be the next to become involved. Sound, projection and lighting designers would follow.

The creative team's input works out from the initial idea under the director's guidance. The different elements of the production become tangible as scripts, scores, models, plans, schedules and sets become available. These are assembled in rehearsal and then in the space where the production is to be performed.

There is a specific sequence to the time in the venue, technical elements are rigged and tested first, then the performers are added. Rehearsals work through all the elements at once and in time until the performances. These rehearsals generally focus on polishing the realisation of the original idea rather than making significant changes to it.

There are two key reasons for this restriction. The first is that the budget might not allow for significant changes and the second is the assumption that the idea, and its realisation, must be broadly correct otherwise it would not have been produced.

Inevitably there are existing, that is not new, works which are being reproduced, re-staged or remounted. Under these circumstances the creative team's scope is more limited than in a totally new work.

However, some works are created not through a linear and chronological process but through the creative team sharing an exploration of ideas. A key component of this process is the freedom to discard work (sometimes including designs) and explore another idea.

Working on the Concept

For me, but I appreciate not for all designers, it is essential at an early stage to acquire information about all the aspects of the production which can limit my work. That is, the nature of the venue, the set and its masking, the production schedule, the budget, the competence of the crew and, the competence of the lighting rental house being used. The sooner I know these factors then the sooner I can learn ways of working within those which are immovable and ways of improving those which can, and need to be, changed.

As I mentioned earlier I like to draw the venue and the set as early as possible so that I have plenty of time to understand the relationship between the two and explore the effect of different positions.

Next, through discussions with the director and set designer, together with script and music studies, I like to establish a design brief, perhaps a synopsis of the cues if they are clear at this point but, if not, at least a description of what the director and set designer saw in their heads when they discussed the set. This brief will also include those ideas which have occurred to me during this stage and, it is important that these ideas are not ruled out because they might be more instinctive than considered.

From this point I begin to work on the plan, addressing those effects which are critical to the production and placing equipment through calculations of both angles and beam spread, deducting this equipment from the stock list so that I know what I have left to play with at each stage.

When I am satisfied that I have covered all the key items known at this point then I will add in the equipment needed for basic actor illumination, my preference being to work in overlapping areas rather than broad washes.

I consider the lighting plan organic so that whilst I might take it to rehearsal or production meetings I can draw on it as different information or ideas develop; it is also useful to demonstrate early ideas to lighting rental houses and electricians.

Get Inside the Script but Don't Take it Too Literally

Lighting designers are usually engaged after the set designer and inevitably after the director. This means that the people in these two positions will almost certainly be more familiar with the script than the lighting designer.

Therefore the lighting designer needs to assimilate the script as quickly as possible, otherwise discussions with other members of the creative team will not be on the same basis.

It is sometimes useful to seek out published material related to the work you are doing to obtain background, but I say 'sometimes' because until you do discuss the piece with the director you do not know if the interpretation will be true to the original. However, the policy of the producer will provide a good clue. For example, I have worked for two opera and one Shakespearean companies who always stayed faithful to the creator's vision so I knew that with these directors none of these productions would be in modern dress, equally that no radical ideas would be introduced.

Let Your Lighting Tell a Story

It is easy to dismiss the main purpose of stage lighting as providing visibility and there is certainly a simple criticality to stage lighting which must be addressed.

However, stage lighting design is about much more, about providing an environment sympathetic to the work, to its setting and development during the performance. It is essential that the lighting designer does not relax having provided good illumination, but continues to work at ensuring the lighting tells a story through its key elements, how it uses direction, colour and intensity to illustrate time, mood and texture.

Playing with Torches

I've always thought that of all the members of the creative team the lighting designer has one of the hardest tasks, simply because most of the others do not need the theatre building in which to demonstrate something of their ideas. The writer can present the script, the composer the score, the set designer the model and the costume designer the drawings and the materials. However, until comparatively recently the lighting designer was obliged to wait until the production was actually in the venue before real lighting ideas could be demonstrated.

It is true that several lighting designers built model theatres in which to try out ideas (myself included) but until small LED light sources model theatre bulbs, fittings and torches simply could not replicate their larger theatre counterparts. Now however, graphic design programs can replicate light beams and even intensities and samples from commercial colour filter and LED ranges and with sufficient accuracy to enable a file of the rendering to then be used to program lighting in the theatre. This helps the lighting designer to demonstrate ideas to the rest of the creative team and potentially make better use of time in the venue itself.

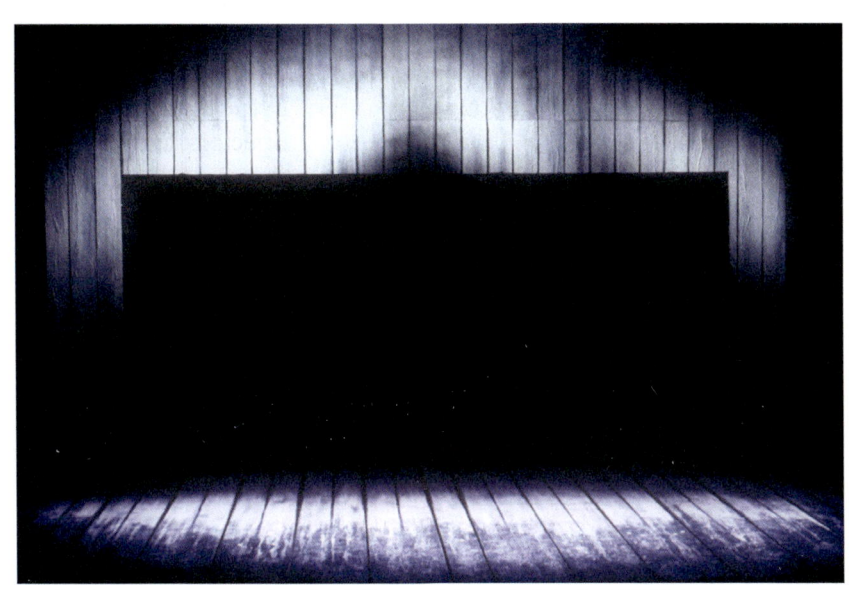

Michael Spencer's setting for Welsh National Opera's 'Macbeth'(1993), a black box which moved up and downstage disgorging witches or collecting bodies as required. Photo Michael Spencer.

Having said this, I recall a situation many years ago when lighting the Welsh National Opera's production of "Macbeth"; the set was designed by an old friend Michael Spencer and consisted of a black box inside a white surround. The key to the production was that the black box moved upstage and downstage on tracks hidden in the white planked floor. What Michael wanted was that no light at all found its way into the black box from which witches would appear as if from nowhere and likewise bodies would disappear as the box moved and seemed to swallow them whole. Michael built a perfectly working big model and we spent an enjoyable and productive afternoon playing just with torches until we arrived at the positions and effects we wanted. Sometimes the cheapest tools are the best!

Work Within or Challenging Limitations

All productions have elements that limit work. Common limitations are time and money but equipment, space and skill are not far behind. Some lighting designers refuse to accept the limitations arguing that the needs of the production must come first. If other members of the creative team feel the same then these powerful forces can bring about fundamental change and, for example, there have been productions when theatres have been remodelled, rehearsal periods extended and previews cancelled. However such productions are rare and most of us work in lesser environments. This does not mean that you should simply give up.

The first priority is to learn what the limitations are and how they affect others. Sometimes trading of budgets or schedules can help different parties. For example, often when it is time for me to focus, some elements of the set are not quite ready; I consider it wiser to give the stage to the crew to address this so that when I do start focusing I'm working on the finished canvas. Sometimes of course this is simply not feasible, the stage floor for example, is often painted overnight to give it time to dry without traffic.

Be Calculating in Unusual Locations

Lighting designers tend to work in very similar venues most of the time, that is, proscenium arch formats, and within a familiar range of (often favourite) equipment.

In these circumstances it is unlikely therefore that lighting designers will need to calculate the intensity that a piece of equipment will deliver in a given situation. It is more likely that they might need to calculate the beam spread for a given throw (although the availability of zoom variable beam equipment makes this less necessary). However, there are circumstances in which calculations are essential and principally these are when the designer is faced with unfamiliar factors. For example when I began designing lighting for the Opera Company of Boston in the USA I had little experience of the US equipment so I calculated throw, beam spread and intensity for each type of light from each position. The result was that I could imagine fairly accurately what the result of each focus would be. When I lit the Bolshoi Ballet at London's Royal Albert Hall in 1993 I did the same exercise because whilst most of the equipment was familiar the throws and angles were not. This hopefully doesn't suggest a formulaic approach to the design but it should free you to experiment with elements from which you know the results.

Power Choice

The power of equipment should relate firstly to the scale of the venue involved and then to the effect required. As the wattage of an instrument increases then there is an inevitable tendency for its physical size and weight to increase too. Consequently, there might be rigging positions which are too small or too frail to accommodate large instruments and smaller, lighter and therefore less powerful instruments might have to be selected instead.

This tends to apply to FOH positions in older theatres and to rigs inserted into 'found' spaces which were not originally designed for performances. In addition, although I have never been obliged to choose lower wattages to lower the room temperature this is an obvious consequence of so doing.

There is also a direct relationship between light output and life expectancy, generally the greater the output at a specific wattage then the lower the life. The implication of this is that a company can be forced into higher running costs simply because the lighting designer selected a high output/low life bulb and I have, notably in 'third-world' countries, often been asked not to do this.

Another factor is the power available at the supply and again this could be lower than desirable in 'found' and temporary spaces. Remember, however, that the limit is the maximum power you want to draw from the supply at any one time and not the maximum power of the whole rig.

The final factor about choosing larger wattage instruments relates to the likely dimmer level at which it will be used. If it turns out to be too powerful then it is likely to spend its life at less than 100% which means that for tungsten units the colour of the beam will be warmer than it would be at 100% and this will have the effect of over-emphasising warmer fillers and dulling the cooler ones. This aspect becomes more complex when instruments are used in which the variation of intensity depends on mechanical shutter devices rather than on the changing of the current.

Moving Lights

There was a time when moving lights could only be afforded by both the largest venues and productions and consequently lighting designers who worked outside these areas could only dream. Today such devices are much more common and it is a rare theatre which doesn't have access to at least a few moving lights; even school theatres are so equipped.

The term 'moving light' requires some explanation. It implies that the light will be moved during the performance whilst the beam is illuminated; whilst this is, of course, perfectly feasible the device can also be used as a remote controllable refocusable spotlight, and in this mode a single moving light can do the work of a battery of conventional lights. This application can save space in the rig and focusing time up the ladder.

The great benefit of moving lights is that they allow the lighting designer to experiment with angles, beam sizes and quality and colour because the more sophisticated lights allow remote control over all these aspects. They allow the lighting designer to respond to the production as it comes together on the stage and, significantly, to support the director's (sometimes new) ideas as he or she comes to terms with what they see in front of them.

Moving lights can take the form of spots which echo the conventional profile/ellipsoidal or, a wash light which echoes the conventional Fresnel. Some moving lights are fitted with framing shutters like conventional profiles/ellipsoidals and most, but not all, provide some degree of colour mixing.

However, moving lights contain considerable numbers of moving parts which increases the risk of breakdown. This means that you need good access to online, local technical help and, spare parts plus a spare unit in stock just in case. These units are not cheap but generally the more expensive are so for a good reason.

Don't Take Lists for Granted

In my experience lists of equipment which the theatre states as being available are rarely accurate; older equipment is often still on the list but is actually waiting repair and newer equipment just hasn't made it on the list yet! If the theatre is close by then a visit can resolve this but at the very least a phone call should be made with this in mind.

This book concentrates on the design and solutions which I have experienced and not on the equipment, which is explained in many books and websites. Nevertheless it might be useful if I clarify my approach to choosing equipment.

I choose equipment first according to what beam control it offers and, second, according to what power I need. In general terms I do not want equipment to produce spill which can catch masking and scenery and produce untidy and distracting blemishes, this means that I tend towards profile spotlights rather than Fresnel or PARS, however PCs offer slightly more control.

It is worth remarking here that the discretion offered by the profile in this respect is only feasible if the lenses are clean!

A balance in choosing equipment is necessary because the degree of control offered by the profile (variable beam angle, peak and flat control, shutter control and the ability to project images) comes at the expense of higher capital or rental charges than other equipment and longer focusing times.

Don't Take Drawings for Granted!

Drawings issued by the theatre and of the theatre should be accurate. This rather obvious statement hints at some disturbing experiences! In one case I was told "Oh! Those flying bars marked on the drawings don't exist, but it shows where we will put them when we have the money!"

As with equipment, visit or phone, don't assume the drawing is recent or up-to-date.

Renew software for drawing annually, cost is a legitimate tax allowance.

Keep Lights Accessible

It's a good idea to draw the rig plan over a copy of the set (and masking) ground plan. As you draw think about how you are going to focus the overhead equipment; can your ladder, Tallescope or Genie get around the set? What happens if the stage floor is raked, stepped or textured?

Lights are often rigged before the set is erected but there is no value in rigging lights if later you can't get to them.

Redraw the Set Plan into Your System

I would strongly advise that you take the set designer's plan and redraw it into your version of the ground plan. Firstly, because this is a simple way of familiarising yourself with the details of the set and secondly because, almost alone, the lighting designer is the most likely person to be affected by and to affect the masking.

The chances are the lighting designer's plan will be the one showing the most elements (that is, venue, set, masking and lighting) and also the most recently drawn. There are benefits to producing the plan everyone consults!

Drawing Plans and Sections

Like most designers of my generation my early lighting plans were hand-drawn using geometric shapes available from school stencils. Then Richard Pilbrow introduced lighting stencils into the UK and suddenly all our plans became more accurate and easier to read. My father, an engraver, also made me stencils of my own which had a few quirks not found on those commercially available and, since they were custom-made, could be engraved with my own name. I sold quite a few of these around my contacts at the time!

Compared to the process today, plans then still had to be drawn by hand, usually on A2 or A1 paper, and taken to a special printers and then delivered or posted to the venue's electricians. Naturally this took some time, especially if the designer was not located in the same town as the venue (and also before the arrival of fax machines).

The advent of personal computers did stimulate some designers to experiment with graphic programs and produce their own symbols, this before commercial lighting design drafting programs were developed. I was however told by the UK company Modelbox, that I was one of the first UK lighting designers to use their CAD system for a lighting design. This was for a national tour of the first authorised stage version of 'Winnie the Pooh'. The set-up time was modest, certainly no longer than it would have taken me to draw by hand, and thereafter I was able to make changes over the telephone and Modelbox would then post the amended plan to next week's venue. At this point the management was reluctant to pay for this service and therefore it came out of my fee, a not inconsiderable percentage in those days which is why I eventually discontinued the process.

Lighting designers are probably unique in the artistic team in the way in which they have to communicate information to others because an essentially imaginative idea has to be translated by the creator into technical language which the creator has fully calculated to be feasible beforehand. Much of this process is undertaken alone.

The ease with which digital images can be produced, altered and transmitted means that several generations of a plan can be issued, as discussion documents, before the final one. Plans should change as more information becomes available, notably through your attendance at rehearsal and through negotiations about the budget and schedule. I like to establish a plan early in the process and use it as developing work in progress. (But if you do this make sure the plans are dated and marked 'Preliminary' and 'Final'). Also make sure, if you are going to send the plan electronically, that the person at the other end has the same drawing program as yourself.

It is wise to include good references on the plans about scales, a simple ratio such as 1:50 is not enough because, as I indicated above, the plan might be reduced or enlarged on a photocopier somewhere in its existence and the ratio no longer applies.

Therefore, when stating the scale also state the size of the plan to which the scale relates such as "1:50 if at A4". Equally add a scale check on the plan: a series of rectangles in alternate lines which indicate (say) 0, 1, 2, 3m and from which the reader can measure other dimensions.

Don't assume the locations of equipment are accurate; the rigging in studio theatres is often designed to be relocated. If a visit is not feasible then a phone call to the head electrician can go some way to detecting if these problems exist; additionally, some theatres also provide photographs on their websites.

Whilst the plan eventually forms the core of the communications between the lighting designer and the crew it should first be used as a kind of technical canvas on which positions and angles can be placed, measured and adjusted. In other words whilst the concept is formed in the designer's head, its realisation begins with the plan.

It is also important to use the plan to check access to the instruments for focusing; there is no point in creating the best rig ever seen if you can't get to it, or, if it takes so long to get to that time runs out and some items aren't focused until well into the plotting. I've often moved cardboard or digital shapes of ladders, genie hoists or Tallescope around plans to check access to lighting positions. Few positions need to be so precise that slight adjustments for access are not acceptable. Consider too the implications for crew who have to climb equipment to undertake your focusing. Are they being asked to place themselves at risk to reach the focus controls?

Other factors which affect how well you work include the degree to which the production desk provides for your needs, from comfort, adequate adjustable lighting, space for all relevant paperwork, good communications and provision for catering, waste paper and appropriate laptops and lighting controls.

Recognising the beneficial affect of these elements, many international lighting designers carry their own desk, especially if they are likely to be in the theatre for many days on the larger shows.

Keep all plans of all shows but notate them afterwards so next time you visit you can be better informed; I also note the names of crew, especially those particularly slow or particularly fast. My notes also include reference to how accurate the rig is located according to my plan, how much of the rig works the first time, how long it takes to focus each lighting position and how quickly the staff can make adjustments on the lighting desk. Time is the lighting designer's biggest enemy so be well armed to face it.

Your Plan is Possibly the Best Yet!

In the days when plans had to be drawn by hand and in ink, changes and/or updates were laborious and rare. In today's world of Computer Aided Design (CAD) revisions can be made quickly and circulated instantly across continents and oceans. Nevertheless it is highly likely that the lighting designer's plans will be the most recently drawn and therefore the most up-to-date. Another useful aspect of lighting designer's drawing is that most LDs draw sections in order to judge lighting angles and masking and consequently once again these are likely to be valuable to other members of the team[1].

How to Inspire a Lighting Designer

As I have said earlier, lighting designers are rarely involved with the very first concept of a production which usually begins with the engagement by the producer of the director, with that of the set designer following closely behind.

Although the first time the lighting designer is introduced, the set may

---

1   2 Essential reading in this area is David Ripley's book "AutoCAD - A Handbook for Theatre Users: 3rd edition" Entertainment Technology Press.

Ming Cho Lee's setting for the Opera Company of Boston's 'Madama Butterfly' (USA premier of the original version 1984). An inspiring and versatile combination of painted abstract and three-dimensional elements, directed by Sarah Caldwell.
Photo Jim deVeer.

still be a shared mental image rather than a sketch or white cardboard model and in reality his or her freedom to make significant changes is already limited. This is perhaps not unreasonable but, light travels in more-or-less straight lines and obeys the laws of physics and therefore it is wise to check with the lighting designer at an early stage that the set does not pose too much of a challenge to these elements. I have been fortunate to light over 500 productions across three continents and yet I have been involved before the set was fixed in fewer than 5% of those cases. (In saying this I would counsel the reader to make a distinction between the levels at which most of us work and those of the mega-musicals which demand and receive both considerably greater resources).

This means that most of the time the canvas on which the lighting designer must paint already contains shapes, textures and colours.

In approaching the piece to be lit lighting designers may already know the story of the production in question. This was true in my case when lighting in Europe and the USA where most of my work was for classical ballet, grand opera or Shakespeare. Conversely, in Australia most of my work is for newly written drama.

This means that it is possible, though not always wise, to make an assumption from the script about the style in which the piece is being presented before the initial discussions with the director and the designer take place.

Such initial assumptions might inform early production meetings where resources are being budgeted.

In Boston, director Sarah Caldwell's policy was to present opera as true to the composer's original music as possible, thus it was my honour to light the USA premiere of Puccini's original version of 'Madame Butterfly'. In addition, whilst Sarah was not above using some contemporary device in her staging, these were not gimmicks and thus it was also possible to assume the opera would be performed in the correct period.

Updating a work to more recent times, in my view, rarely works if the philosophies being expressed through the libretto remain fixed in an earlier age. Opera buffs are often accustomed to enjoying the production with their eyes firmly closed!

Before writing about how Sarah briefed me for 'Butterfly' it will be helpful for me to explain my working method for her company. During the season I commuted across the Atlantic every three weeks, always leaving Boston the day after the opening night, on this day Sarah and I would meet and, with the set model in front of us, she would talk through her ideas for the next opera. I would then receive plans in London just before flying back to Boston, where I would embark on a melange of watching rehearsal, set construction and plan drawing. All this took place in the Opera House itself, the company lacking either rehearsal or workshop facilities elsewhere for most of its life.

Sarah was not only the director of the productions but also artistic director of the company and, significantly for the lighting designer, also the conductor, which simply means she was unable to see the lighting from any perspective except that from the orchestra pit. Consequently our discussions were confined to the original chat and then occasional comments shouted above the orchestra. Her dry wit kept all of us on our toes; "Puccini is dead – follow me!"

Briefing me, Sarah asked if I knew how 'Butterfly' had come to be written, I didn't. She explained that the composer, Puccini, had been in London and had seen a play about a woman who had met a sailor with whom she had a child but the sailor had left her. One day the sailor's ship is seen in harbour and the woman waits all night for him to come to her. The play's producer was David Belasco, a noted US stage genius, and Mr Belasco had produced a sequence of sunset, moon rise and set, and sunrise, all with primitive electric light and no action or dialogue. Sarah then said to me: "Puccini was so moved by the lighting he then wrote the opera – it's all yours!"

The opera contains this sequence with music and chorus offstage and is a tour de force for a lighting designer, matching lighting to the mood and timing of the music and of the piece. Such sequences might be inspired by real events but on stage some theatricality is needed. I watched rehearsals to see where Butterfly stood (upstage centre) and where she looked (down into the harbour). Then I decided the sun would set stage right which meant the moon would appear stage left then move stage right followed by the sun rising stage left. The lights were rigged at different heights to create the sinking or rising of the source and the colours changed to also reflect the rise and fall. Then I plotted the changes into a sequence visually before adjusting it to the music. Sarah then inspected and fortunately made few changes. I'm happy to say it was a much talked about sequence.

It seems to me that no matter how long one works in theatre and especially in lighting there are still moments which send a chill down one's spine, moments when the elements come together, live, right in front of you. I had this experience recently in a production for the Spare Parts Puppet Theatre in Australia when a storm sequence just clicked. I had thrown patches of dark grey-purple clouds onto the cyc and at one rehearsal their lighting cue happened just as a threatening piece of new music was introduced. The two matched perfectly, but neither I nor the brilliant composer Lee Buddle had discussed this moment; we were simply each responding to the script and the drama.

4 ON STAGE

Do You Have Everyone's Contacts?

A good production manager will issue a list of all the people involved in the production and their contact details but this doesn't always happen, so, make sure you pass on your contacts and in return obtain those of the key people with whom you are working. You might not need them on the current production but they might well be useful in the future.

Budgets and Schedules

Lighting budgets cover the cost of providing equipment (usually rented), purchasing colour filters, special effects, and can include electrical props. If you use these elements sparingly then your client will notice (especially if you get good results) and is therefore more likely to use you again. Your economy however, should be a bonus of your design rather than its sole objective. UK lighting designer and author, the late Francis Reid, has written that it is unwise to manipulate figures just to make the total look good. Budgets, he said, should be realistic otherwise what is the point of having them?

Certainly early budgets, when there are likely to be many unknowns, should include high contingencies. I also like to keep an eye on the budgets of my colleagues to explore moving the money around.

Like budgets, schedules are simply the best informed guess about the sequence and timing of events to come. They are organic in that forces outside the control of the person who created the schedule can force changes to be made. I keep records of how long it takes me to focus different parts of the rig in the theatres in which I work (and importantly which technicians were involved). This helps me to plan for later focus sessions or even for future visits.

One key aspect is whether the set is actually ready for focusing and I often keep an eye on the fit-up and offer to give up some of my focus time if this will help the set to be more completed for focusing.

Just like budgets schedules need a contingency, in units of time rather than currency. It is better to be ahead rather than behind and beneficial to have time to experiment and refine.

Production Meetings

These meetings of both creative and technical people are critical and need to be held regularly and minuted. They need to be held around all relevant models, drawings, budgets and schedules so that all parties can work from the same, and most recent, information.

Be Green

Theatre consumes considerable resources in time, people, materials and power. The cost of some of these factors can be controlled through careful planning but experimentation and improvisation are key components of the theatre art and need to be budgeted accordingly. The lighting designer's equipment can be expensive to hire, rig and light up so it is helpful to the production if waste can be kept to a minimum.

The increasingly large numbers of LED lights offer considerable savings through reduced power, air conditioning and maintenance and most manufacturers offer data to help calculate the potential savings.

Masking

It's axiomatic that a lighting designer needs to know where the masking is going before the lighting rig plan can begin. Often the initial set model and ground plan will not show the positions or even the existence of masking.

There are, essentially, two types of masking: the more traditional wings and borders which provide gaps for the movement of actors and scenery (and lighting too) and more continuous masking which wraps around the sides and rear of the stage (also requiring borders overhead).

This latter version, whilst often intruding less into the horizontal sightline than would wings, can impede the movement of actors and certainly prevents the use of low sidelight from the wings. Key lighting positions in this format are from the downstage corners where hopefully there is space for a good tower of lights well masked by a tormentor.

Masking is provided to hide the backstage paraphernalia and create a neutral background against which the performance can take place. In this context it is highly unlikely that the masking would be lit. However, masking can not only conceal but also form part of the set or at least, provide a sympathetic scenic frame in which the set sits. In this case it is likely that the lighting designer will need to light the wings and borders.

In this latter situation a number of factors have to be taken into account including whether the texture of the elements needs to be enhanced (in which case the light should strike the surface at an acute angle, creating highlights and shadows) or, whether the masking has some fullness or creases which need to be hidden (in which case the light should strike the surface as close to 90° as is feasible. For example, black masking can be made from a variety of fabrics but usually velour (velvet) or wool, but velour has a nap, a raised texture, which will look different under different angles of light, whereas wool is usually flat and will not. Finally, consideration needs to be made about how stray light disappears beyond the masking and into wings and flies. Generally, borders can be lit from positions on proscenium booms just above head height and where the spill will disappear into the fly tower. Wings can be lit from overhead bars where the spill disappears off stage.

Lighting designers prefer hard masking to soft drapes, or at least prefer drapes to have no fullness. This is because the folds can catch stray light and be distracting. Hard masking can also be set at an angle whereby the offstage edge is set to light upstage to avoid the widening beam of crosslight.

Who Does the Masking?

Rigging deadlines can frequently require the lighting designer to take an initiative and liaise with the set designer firstly about overall masking policy – are the lights to be visible or not – then moving on to consider the need for entrances before masking elements can be drawn.

Set designers understandably often prefer their work to be seen against a clean surround. I have found that early discussions with the set designer can often resolve masking issues. For example when I was lighting Handel at Sadler's Wells in London the late UK designer Peter Rice climbed a ladder and helpfully pruned a border of real tree branches to let through light from the lights rigged above!

Generally in theatres possessing flying systems, once the rig is in place but before the focusing can begin, the lighting designer has to set a height for the lighting rig, a process known as 'deading' or 'trimming'. This process also includes the lighting designer setting a height for any overhead masking if its function is to obscure both the lighting and the backstage areas from the public.

Peter Rice's clever setting for Handel Opera at Sadler's Wells London, directed by Tom Hawkes. An economical solution using standard black wings and borders but with carefully positioned pillars, trees and drapes.

Herein lies an interesting factor about roles and responsibilities because designing and providing the masking is not part of the lighting designer's job; however, unless the overhead and side masking form part of the set it usually falls to the lighting designer to determine both where they are hung or positioned and how far on stage they come to frame the picture.

Naturally the set designer should be consulted about this; generally set designers prefer masking to be as far offstage as possible so that their set sits within an environment which has clean lines around it. Equally, generally lighting designers might not prefer this arrangement because it pushes the overhead bars higher and steepens angles of light (especially onto faces where the eyes become less visible). These factors can be discussed in advance so when the masking is being set there are no surprises.

Should the Lights be Visible or Not?

This question shows its age because over the years I have been lighting set design has become more exciting about how it relates to its surroundings and the visibility (or not) of the technical elements such as the lighting rig.

I have lit numerous productions in which the producer sometimes wanted an open stage with an industrial feel, but then objected to obligatory intrusions such as exit signs. It is often wiser (but admittedly not cheaper) to design a backstage set so that the creative team have more control.

In terms of lighting there have been significant changes too about whether the audience can see the actual lights. In past decades this was a key question at early design meetings and I should clarify that the concept of the production was not always a clue. This is a basic matter for the lighting designer because visible lights have fewer obstructions from masking but can also often dazzle the audience. I think this is one reason why a lot of lighting designers influenced the positions and types of masking. Lighting designers need to draw vertical sections for this reason and often they are the only members of the creative team doing this.

Rehearsals

There are two types of rehearsal which involve the lighting designer: those (generally) outside the theatre building during which the moves and interpretations are developed and, those later in the theatre and on stage during which the technical elements are added into the production.

In the case of the former I have sometimes been asked by a director not to attend too early in the process until either he or she has had time to think about the lighting or, until the actors become more comfortable with their moves and words.

In productions where improvisation and experiment are central to development there is a risk that attending some, but not regular, rehearsals will provide a patchy and inaccurate picture of the work. Conversely, working in Perth, Western Australia with director the late Alan Becher I have often been asked to join rehearsals and help place actors where they can be more tightly lit. Thank you Alan.

Despite design discussions, script study and the development of cue synopsis lighting designers should attend rehearsals with an open mind so that the natural points and types of cues emerge from the performance itself. Ideally a designer should attend several rehearsals, testing early plans and cue synopsis against the developing production.

The second type of rehearsal, that of adding the technical elements, has become more complex over the years as digital equipment enables sophisticated effects to be produced and changed more easily during rehearsals on stage.

This is a considerable relief to most lighting designers because formal plotting of the lighting sessions rarely involved actors or costumes thus distorting key elements of the picture. In this situation lighting the set became more prominent and lighting levels were unrealistic and had to be changed on the following rehearsal when actors arrived. Directors often used the technical time to experiment with blocking but often at the expense of other trades who needed the stage.

It is a far better use of everyone's time if the lighting designer can add an hour or so onto the end of the focus and plot some general states and test out tricky ones, that is without the director, so that there is a basis for a plot at the technical rehearsal.

At this rehearsal the production will stop several times and an efficient designer, working in conjunction with a fast lighting desk (not always a given) and a sympathetic board operator/programmer can plot several cues and modify others, continuously working over the rehearsal as the actors move around the set. Another factor is that the technical rehearsal is often the first time that the lighting designer will have heard music and sound effects and therefore can time cues accordingly.

Whatever the pressures, it is vital to get out of the venue so that you can give your eyes a rest; on return some previously hidden glitches can become obvious. Work towards gradual but stable improvements at each rehearsal rather than trying to achieve perfection all at once.

Safety, Insurance and Instructions

Most countries have legislation which addresses responsibilities for managing a safe working environment and, whilst the details and depth vary from country to country, essentially the legislation requires that hazards are identified and the risks they impose reduced or eliminated. There are specific responsibilities for designers.

This aspect of designers' work was debated at length in the UK in the 1990s when I chaired a national body charged with the responsibility of producing competence-based qualifications for backstage (i.e. non-performing) personnel. A consensus was reached that designers can request and advise but since they are not (usually) the line managers for stage crew then they can have no direct responsibility for (in the case of lighting) the structural or electrical integrity of their design. Since these deliberations in the 1990s the more recent obligation on designers to carry public liability insurance brings the execution of the designer's role into sharper focus.

For example, as lighting designer you have a right to assume that the equipment you specify and the rig which supports it, will have structural and electrical integrity. Whilst the prime responsibility for this will be that of the head/master electrician and/or the rental company and/or the venue, the designer might be included in a legal action arising from an accident involving the lighting rig, so some insurance is wise (it is also now a condition of contracts in several countries).

The designer must deliver a design which is in itself, inherently safe. In lighting terms this means that the designer must carry out an assessment of the risks the lighting design itself poses. Whilst I think this should include an avoidance of physical and electrical overloads it is more likely to include an assessment of the effects of, for example, stroboscopic, ultra-violet and laser effects, not only on the audience but also on the crew and the performers. I would also include in this section an assessment of dazzling lights or sudden blackouts, especially where there is a subsequent movement of scenery and/or actors. Note that lighting designers generally do not work at heights or rig or connect equipment (but this might be the case if a lighting designer was also the master or chief electrician with different responsibilities.)

Involving the Crew

The process of creating theatre depends on an interesting dilemma in that whilst its creative components originate from people working alone the realisation of their ideas is collaborative.

This applies to lighting design in that whilst I might create the design, decide what lights to put where, and where to aim them and, in what colours, I need other people to actually hang the lights, plug them in and point them. Even more I rely on someone to program the lighting desk.

I have found it wise to involve the crew and the programmer in my thinking for a number of reasons. Firstly there is a good chance they have worked in the theatre you are in more than you have and might have encountered and solved some of its physical problems before. Secondly, the production you are doing might be touring later and unless the producer is engaging you to relight it at each date (which is rare) maybe the master electrician or programmer is scheduled to undertake this task. Therefore, in this latter case especially, the more they are following your thinking the more they can interpret your design in other locations where circumstances might be challengingly different.

The Stage is Yours – Focusing

The comments above assume that the time allowed in the production schedule for focusing and then for plotting, is realistic in the first place and this might not be the case if the lighting designer has had little opportunity to help put the production schedule together or at least to comment before it was issued.

In this respect it is critical that the lighting designer is made aware of what time constraints are fixed and what are negotiable.

For example, in the case of focusing there are a number of predetermined elements which influence how fast, or how slow, the focus will take. These can be summarised as:

Items which can slow the focus:
- Untrained crew, unfamiliar with the venue and equipment;
- Faulty equipment, inaccurate rigging and patching;
- Inadequate access equipment;
- Raked, stepped or uneven stage surfaces;
- A rig which consists mainly of profiles/ellipsoidals;
- focusing which requires scenery;
- Tight focusing of very specific items.

Items which can speed the focus:
- Trained crew, familiar with the venue and equipment;
- Efficient equipment, accurate rigging and patching;
- Access equipment which is safe and can reach where needed;
- Flat and even stage surface;
- A rig which consists of few profiles/ellipsoidals;

- focusing which does not require scenery;
- focusing which forms part of a wash.

Naturally these elements tend to occur as a mix of slow and fast but at their extremes the time taken to focus one lamp could vary from one minute to 15. If there are 60 luminaires in the rig then the time needed to complete the focus would thus also vary considerably. However, all the above elements are known in advance and, the time allowed in the schedule for the focus is also known and therefore these factors can be interactive with the size of the rig and the nature of the positions and equipment chosen.

That is, if the time allowed for the focus is fixed then there is little point in designing a rig with so much equipment that there is insufficient time for it to be focused.

The production schedule should be treated as everyone's best estimate of what they would like to see happen and it should be regarded as organic so that it can be changed and refined as new information becomes available. This process should continue during the fit-up. I certainly monitor the work of other departments and adjust my stage time if that helps other departments to complete items I need such as scenery, masking or floor painting.

An assessment of where to start focusing needs to be made in terms of minimising the crew's workload. I tend to start with those positions which are the hardest to reach and work towards the easier locations so that, as the crew tire, then their tasks become easier and thus the quality of their work (and the rate at which they achieve it) should remain constant.

Alternatively, you can start with the trickiest items to focus or with those shots you are not quite sure of so that if some things don't quite work out you will have time to make changes from the simpler elements in the rig.

Operators – the Doorway to Your Design

The title or job description of the person who plots the lighting into the lighting control system has changed over the decades. In the UK this person used to be known as the 'board op' in other words the operator of the (lighting) switchboard. Today 'programmer' is more common reflecting the computer technology involved. With this change of title has come a change in responsibility. It used to be that the lighting designer needed to know how various lighting control systems worked in order to couch plotting instructions in the most helpful manner. It is not that modern control systems make this unnecessary, designers should always have regard for how they work with their programmers, but today it is more that designers should discuss the effect required and rely on the programmer to work out the process.

Cheating

A cheat sheet is a colloquial term for any shorthand notes or sketches which a lighting designer creates for themselves to help them plot the production. These can be hard copy on paper or more likely on a laptop or tablet (provided that it is backed up).

There are distinct advantages in taking the time to create such paperwork. For example, the drawing of the lighting rig, whilst containing much of the information needed for plotting, is likely to take up most of the production desk at A1 or A2 sizes whereas a cheat sheet can be A4, sit comfortably on the production desk next to the script and other data and, be designed to be read in low light conditions. A lighting plan will also lack information about the script and the cues but a cheat sheet can contain any data required.

There is no right or wrong way to draw up a cheat sheet, whatever works for you is acceptable. I tend to draw schematic layouts of the set and then add block arrows which are placed on the sketch at the centre of where the light falls, the direction of the arrow tells me from which direction the light is coming. Once I have completed the focus then I go back over the dimmer channels one by one and write in the arrow its channel number.

There are several by-products of this process. Firstly, if the sketch and its arrows are accurate I can quickly see if one part of the stage is better served than another.

Secondly, by flashing through the channels immediately at the end of the focus (but before plotting) I can check if I've missed any instruments. Thirdly, I can check if they are all still in the correct place and if something has been knocked whilst other work is taking place. Finally, if the director is present at this 'flash-through' then it is a useful opportunity for them to learn what the lighting designer has to work with.

A cheat sheet only exists to simplify information so that the lighting designer can work more efficiently. If it begins to resemble a map of a railway junction then it's time to go back to the drawing board. (Interestingly I wonder as I write that phrase if in today's digital world this means anything to the younger generation!)

Assessing Lighting Changes

There are two main visual components to the lighting of a production, the pictures themselves and the way in which one picture changes into another.

Terminology is important, each picture can be called a cue, a state, a preset, a set-up, a memory; most of these terms have entered the lighting designer's patois because they describe operational aspects of control systems. In stage management terms the moment of changing from one picture to the next is usually called a cue, its position in the script sometimes known as the cue-point.

In looking at the both the pictures and the way they change and assessing whether they work or not the judgement must take into account whether the following are appropriate for the desired effect:

- the instruments selected for use in the cue;
- the colour and focus of the selected instruments;
- the relative balance of the selected instruments;
- the in and out times allocated to the fades;
- the point in the script or action when the cue takes place.

The five elements listed above are interdependent. Thus, changes to one will affect all the others. Of special importance is the point at which the cue takes place and a judgement of the picture and critically of the in and out fades cannot be made without also judging if the change is happening in the most appropriate place in the script or the action. The plotted state might be perfect but the cue-point wrong or vice versa. If you're not sure where the problem lies then it is easier and wiser to try the cue earlier or later before you tamper with the recorded state.

Apart from obvious lighting changes which involve house lights and set or curtain dressing there are only two types of lighting change, those which the lighting designer intends the audience to notice and those which are not evident but act on the audience subliminally.

The former will usually be associated with some action, set change and/or music change and are therefore likely to take both their timing and position from one of these elements external to the lighting itself.

The latter is usually a device which the lighting designer wishes to employ to influence the mood or attention of the audience, perhaps by subtle changes of colour, perhaps by gently increasing the contrast between the focal point of the action and the surrounding area. Subliminal cues are usually very slow and, in order to smooth out the change and make it unnoticeable, might involve several stages and adjustments to the profile of the fade.

Sometimes one instrument becomes uncomfortably more prominent than others during an incoming fade. The solution to this is to either adjust the profile of the fade on that dimmer, if the control system will permit this, or to simply 'pre-heat' this instrument in the preceding state by giving the dimmer channel a low level, 5% to 10% - so that, whilst it's intensity is too low for the light to be visible, the filament will nevertheless already be warm and it will therefore increase its intensity more smoothly.

It's Not What We Had Before!

Before the days of computer memory lighting controls, when operators were obliged to manually set and reset faders, there was a certain inevitability that human error would creep into the settings and the resultant stage picture not look as it once did. In such situations it was understandable that directors lost a degree of faith in the lighting team's ability and would loudly comment "that's not what we had before!". Directors have astonishing memories for the details of a production and it is worth not overreacting to this criticism but stopping to consider what might have happened.

Whilst the development of memory lighting controls has made this situation far less likely, human error is still inevitable, so this cry can still be heard but now it requires some interpretation. I have learned that the director is more likely to mean "I don't like what I'm seeing today". The value of memory controls is that yesterday's picture can be saved, recalled for comparison with a new version.

Another modern aid is the video of the rehearsal or plotting session which enables everyone to check what happened previously. It is unlikely however that unless the equipment is broadcast quality that the image would be reliable as to intensities and colour values but nevertheless the video would still provide evidence of actor and set moves and lighting cue point and durations.

Breaks and Eye Strain

For a lighting designer breaks not only provide opportunities for improving physical and mental comfort but they provide critical opportunities to rest the eyes. This is especially important when light levels are low because inevitably the length of time it takes to plot will be longer than the length of time the audience will be exposed to that lighting cue and therefore the lighting designer's perception will be different from that of the audience. Getting out of the theatre and then seeing the relevant cue soon after returning will provide a more realistic sensation of what the audience will experience. The same goes for any aspect of lighting, colour choice, cue speeds and the focus. Seeing your work afresh is very important and this is unlikely if you rarely leave the stalls!

What Happens if You are Unwell?

If you become ill you might be so incapacitated that you are unable to continue lighting the production. This has happened to me thankfully only once in a long career but you might wish to take note of what I learned.

If you are likely to be ill, feel unwell or suffer from a recurring illness identify someone who can take over from you and whom the management would accept as your deputy.

Keep your notes up to date so that someone can take over immediately and not lose time trying to catch up. Keep these notes, and all your other data, in a ring binder and let the management know where you keep it.

If you are so ill that you are unable to return to the production, discuss with the management a press release which identifies the role and credit of your deputy.

What is a Lighting Design?

As I mentioned above, some years ago I was taken ill during plotting and my assistant had to finish the show for me. A disturbing experience this. When we later discussed the tour he felt he should be credited for the lighting design; I felt that since I had designed the rig, focused it and at least started the plot I should be credited also. He argued that he had made a few changes to the rig so he was the designer. In the end we amicably agreed to share the credit but the question remains, what is the lighting design? I can't be just the rig, nor just the focus nor just the plot. Perhaps too as a set designer from the Bolshoi said to me once "design is idea!"

I'm interested in the influences on the final design and what role these influences have on the ownership.

I once arrived at a regional venue on the usual cold Monday tour date to find there had been some miscommunication and the lighting rig and not been done. There was no time to catch up and I had to use the rig left over from the previous Sunday's 'Gang Show', basically strong colour washes. Our set was white and designed to change colour but the range was far stronger than ideal. Interestingly however it worked very well and I learned a lesson. But the result at that venue was not all my work.

If the rig is defined as a key part of the design then when the rig is predetermined by the venue and not the designer does that mean a different assessment is required of the ownership? The only show I ever lit at the Royal Opera House in London (pre-upgrade) had pre-focused and pre-coloured FOH. I had no choice but to use it but it wasn't quite what was needed. In the great days of variety at the London Palladium the standing rig (designed by the legendary Bill Platt) served visiting Sunday concerts extremely well.

Every lighting designer has worries about his or her work when encountering such trials as rusty equipment, patchy schedules or cancelled flights. The anticipation of problems can be reasonable risk management, but sometimes this goes too far. I once saw a programmer disappear into the lighting box with two bottles of Tequila and was more than slightly disturbed. Curiously he turned out to anticipate my instructions very accurately. Hmmm, maybe I should have been worried if he hadn't any supplies!

Overcoming these challenges maintains the integrity of the initial design but sometimes meeting the challenge is such an exercise in itself that this takes over from delivering the final result. When I lit 13 ballets in repertoire for the Bolshoi's London Royal Albert Hall season the logistics (no refocusing and two crew) took me over completely and once the rig was focused and working I caught myself relaxing with relief but then realised I hadn't actually plotted the show yet!

Our design, however it is defined, is, of course, put through a filter over which we have little control (voltage fluctuations for example). On one of my shows the stage manager nervously whispered to the board op "that's a snap blackout!" came the board op's reply, "I'm doing it, I'm doing it!"

5 TIPS

Stage Etiquette

Most stages are very accessible in the sense that no keys are required to access them from elsewhere in the theatre building. This means that anyone in that theatre building can simply walk on to the stage and colonise it. Given that this is the major workspace some discipline is needed if safety and efficiency are to be preserved. It is wise to think of the stage as a possession to be courteously borrowed and returned to its management who would ensure it is available and properly set up for the task in hand. Respect also means not talking when others are concentrating, not bringing drinks onto the stage once it is set, and not moving furniture and props off their marks without replacing them.

How Tidy is the Theatre?

It is inevitable that you will be asked to light a production in a theatre in which you've never worked before and consequently it is also inevitable that you will be uncertain about how good is its the equipment and its crew. Of course, you might know some people who have worked there who you can ask, but one arbiter I have used which has never failed me, is a glance around at how clean and tidy the stage is – the level of efficiency and competence relates directly to that of the care with which the crew treat their workplace.

Move About

It is normal and universal that the lighting designer sits in the middle of the auditorium at a production desk in order to watch rehearsal and plot the lighting cues. This location is perhaps the best from which to watch the performance but there are many other viewing positions! Each of these provides a slightly differing view of the stage and consequently of the lighting.

For example, if the theatre has more than one level then seats on higher levels will see more of the stage floor. It is wise therefore of the lighting designer to watch different rehearsals from different parts of the auditorium and then to allow time to make slight adjustments.

I was once asked to go to the US from the UK to light a play called 'Crimes of the Heart' featuring three actresses on a three-sided thrust stage. The director told me she had blocked the play so that each actress featured more strongly on one side than on another and asked that I reflect this in the lighting. I complied, but with some scepticism about this actually working. I was wrong, as I moved around the theatre I saw the play each time in a differing perspective. Of course the audience couldn't move but the publicity said 'come three nights see three productions!'

Keep Some Up Your Sleeve

However well you plan, however well you understand the production, there will always be occasions when you need an extra light, maybe to try an idea that has been stimulated by the rehearsals or maybe because there is a hole in the cover. Therefore, I always include in my rigs extra lights for which I have no clear purpose when I draw the plan but which are there to fill those unexpected moments. I generally choose profiles/ellipsoidals for these and locate them centrally front of house and centrally downstage; they need to be allocated dimmers at the same time as all other lights are so they are always immediately ready to use. In small rigs this might seem like a waste of resources but I have rarely found they are redundant! However, when you draw them on your plan use your own shorthand. I used to label them 'spares' and have sometimes caught the director studying the plan and presenting me with his or her ideas for the use of 'my' spares!

Costumes and Colour

Lighting designers should be able to view the costume designs at an early stage in the production and, more importantly, be able to make comments, especially on the potential impact of any strong colours. For example, I have been faced in opera with black sopranos in a black costume against a black background and on another occasion white sopranos in white costumes against white backgrounds. Whilst our job can sometimes be to make people 'disappear' it is usually the reverse and therefore a level of contrast between background and foreground (actors) in the design is valuable. In the above cases the sopranos were the stars and therefore located centre stage but one occasion a star in a white costume on a white set had chorus around and behind her with each chorus member costumed in bright colours.

The scene was supposed to be set in bright sun. Consequently there was a risk that the attention of the audience would go to the bright chorus around the edges and not to the washed out white clothed star! I had no input into the set or costume design which were both fixed before I was engaged and the only option I had was to pull down the light off the chorus and add key light onto the star. It lacked the feeling of the time of day but the star was visible!

Establish a File for Relights

A large part of a lighting designer's job involves relighting productions either on tour or as a revival in a new season of work. There are two challenging aspects to this. Firstly, reproducing one's lighting from an earlier season often requires a high level of accurate recording of plans, patching, focus and plotting because many elements might be key to the action.

However, the opportunity to make alterations and improvements is very tempting. Actors and stage crew often base actions on lighting positions and changes so adjustments which might seen innocent can have repercussions! These days the ability to record video at good quality is a major asset in relighting and I work with several companies which use this method and get the creative team to watch the recording and discuss what to keep and what to change.

It's unwise to discard old plans and files of productions because you might be asked to light it again and you might work in that venue again. Additionally lighting designers are often asked to teach and their material is very useful to demonstrate what was actually done rather than the theory. If productions are significant, or the lighting designer becomes significant, their material is often donated to universities or libraries for others to study.

Slowly But Surely, Gradual Improvements

I know lighting designers who spend a great deal of time in the focusing and plotting stages to ensure that everything is as accurate as it can be at that time. I have nothing against this approach but I prefer to treat the realisation phase of the production as more organic, almost sketching in focuses and cues so that as the various elements come together I have time and room to manoeuvre, polish and refine. One critical aspect, which is repeated in this book, is that you simply cannot judge a lighting cue accurately until it is operated in the correct place in the action, and this might require several adjustments until it is in the correct place.

Keep It Clean!

I was lucky to be trained as a lighting designer by the venerable UK lighting designer and author Francis Reid. Francis warned of 'muddy' thinking which, he said, produces 'muddy' lighting!

We Can Only Work at Night

Open air venues usually lack the level of sophistication in their facilities that are enjoyed by their indoor counterparts and this can adversely affect the audience's expectation of and reaction to the performance.

Consequently the very novelty of doing the piece outdoors, perhaps in a specially relevant location, must be itself a selling point to prevent the audience making comparisons. The lighting can help here by allocating resources to dress the overall site in addition to the stage and thus placing the performing area into a vernal context.

Organisations loaning or renting out lights generally like to know if they are going to be located in a situation where they might be placed at risk and, dependent upon the local weather, this naturally occurs in the case of an outdoor production. Rental companies, or technicians associated with outdoor venues, usually know very well which lights resist rain damage and which don't.

Sadly and frequently this means that older lights will be more available than expensive new ones and in turn this means that shutters might be past their best and equally the light output might have to struggle to reach the stage in any strength. Another factor relevant to using lights outdoors is the range of temperatures acting upon light bulbs which can cause them to blow if initially used too quickly. This is especially the case at the higher wattages and often these occur too in projection equipment. It is wise to gently warm up the bulbs first before the audience are allowed in the venue.

Part of this process should also include a check that the lights are still focused where the lighting designer intended because many outdoor venues lack permanent rigging positions and some venues are used by the general public during the day so it is easy for lights to get knocked. I speak from bitter experience; on one outdoor production I lit much of the rig was refocused daily by the local peacocks that lived in the amphitheatre!

Many outdoor venues are not located close to city centres and therefore closed to public transport. While this will inevitably pose a problem for an audience, it will also pose a problem for crew getting home after late-night calls and therefore the production budget might need to cater for taxis. Perhaps too the venue lacks proximity to fast food outlets and so some catering needs to be provided on site. Some sites might be plagued by mosquitoes. Whilst these aspects of a production are the responsibility of the production manager and not the lighting designer, nevertheless a wise designer checks that measures are in place to keep his or her crew happy.

Another, presumably obvious, problem with working outdoors is that – alone in the company – the lighting designer can't work until it goes dark. Assuming that he or she would prefer not to be working regularly at 3am (and in any case balancing lights needs actors and they have union rules) then it follows that especially in outdoor productions designers have to be very efficient in the use of their time. Not for the first time then, this requires clear thinking about what the lights are doing and clear thinking produces clear lighting. Also not for the first time, in this situation it is essential that the lighting control is so easy to operate that it doesn't waste valuable time – because much plotting will be done over technical and dress rehearsals.

The hour of darkness in outdoor lighting terms really means the time at which the stage lights begin to register stronger than twilight. Here, it is important to be aware that the twilight, the half light, occupies different time-scales across the world, so whilst at the equator twilight virtually doesn't exist, closer to the poles even darkness might not be total at some times of the year.

A local meteorological office or observatory should be able to provide sunset times for the relevant site and, of course, since these times occur twice each year, if the production is planned early enough then it is possible to visit the site on the first to judge the effect on the second. A true story: on my first major outdoor production in the UK I went to the new computerised meteorological office to learn the sunset times. They were unable to help pinpoint the times at the venue and sent me to a little old lady in a country cottage who, surrounded by crumbling books, accurately gave me the information!

Inextricably linked with the hour of darkness is the hour at which street lights, advertisements and residential areas switch on their own lights and a wise lighting designer will visit the venue several times across several evenings to judge the effect that all these will have on his or her own lighting. This 'ambient' lighting might cast a direct beam onto the stage, or be bright enough to be distracting to an audience because it is located in their general sightline. On some productions, if this is checked early enough, it is possible to relocate the stage to a more secluded part of the site or to plan for the construction of masking pieces.

It's All in the Music

If you are designing lighting for a piece with music it helps if you can read the music but it is not essential. The person cueing the show should be able to do so and should be sitting at the production desk whilst you are plotting. When I lit at Boston Opera the person sitting beside me and cueing the production also cued the surtitles of the translations projected over the proscenium arch; in fact, this person, the late and much missed Dr Lisi Oliver was usually responsible for the translations too and learned many languages during productions!

You can learn about the structure of musical forms, for example songs tend to start with an introduction, then change to the verse, then again change to the chorus, back to the verse, then to the bridge (or 'middle eight') then back again to verse and chorus before the end piece (often known as the 'outro'). On this basis alone there are opportunities for nine lighting changes and if the work includes dance then the music and action should provide more opportunities.

Extra Ideas Need Extra Time – Effects

If the production you are lighting is to include elements which are not usually part of the everyday, such as effects or projection, then it is wise to allow extra time to deal with them. Do not assume you can rig, focus and plot these items in the same time you will be doing the main lighting.

Projection

Projection is a subject on its own and there are several excellent books on the subject so I hope the reader won't mind if I don't go into detail here. A complication is that the speed of technology quickly renders much of written matter redundant. When I wrote my book on projection the main projection medium was slides and digital projection had not then been invented. Despite technological advances I would, however offer three tips which won't age:

- Experiment in advance
- Allow extra time for projection
- Keep light off the screen.

Sunrise and Sunsets

Some years ago I was asked to light an opera in which the action took place in a Mediterranean location during a sunset. The director and designer visited the location and returned with many photographs directing me to simply copy their photographs. My crew and I concentrated hard on choosing authentic colour filters and lighting angles onto the sky cloth. The director and designer were pleased but the major national newspaper review said: "Graham Walne has perpetrated the most tasteless sunset we have ever seen!" On another occasion (also mentioned elsewhere in this book) the director and I sat up on a hill in Boston USA watching the sunset in order to reproduce it in the opera. What I learned from these experiences was that sometimes realism doesn't work on stage; it needs to be theatrical and take cues from the dialogue and action.

Painted Sets

The art of scene painting is now less common than in past centuries but there are still productions which utilise this technique. I have certainly been lucky enough to work in the USA with two legendary practitioners: Herbert Senn and Helen Pond. They came with a formidable reputation, to an extent justifiable because of their immense talent which included

Herbert Senn and Helen Pond's setting (and stunning scene painting) for the Opera Company of Boston's 'Don Pasquale' (1987). Directed by Sarah Caldwell.

magical scenic artistry, and whose work was so realistic that entering theatre from the back of the auditorium it was impossible to tell what was a flat painted surface and what was three dimensional. Herbert and Helen were (understandably) very sensitive about how their painted sets were to be lit; after all, they had chosen the colours and created the shadows but I didn't think I was there simply for illumination, considering that moods and emphasis changes over the performance. I achieved a result they welcomed and initially they couldn't work out how I had created the effect. The answer was straight on flat soft focus breakup gobos (patterns) from the balcony rail in gentle colours which were found in the painting.

Shadows

Every time you switch on a light it will produce a shadow of whatever object the beam hits. If the shadow is distracting it can be tempting to wash it out with another light, but this risks adding another shadow! The best approach is to design the shadows as well as the lighting and make sure they fall where you need them.

Since light travels in straight lines (unless that is it is refracted in some

Herbert Senn and Helen Pond's masterful piece of scene painting, the image is totally flat but with the combination of H&H's painting (and may I say my dapples) a very old battered drop looks good. 'Norma' Opera Company of Boston, (1983). Directed by Sarah Caldwell.

way) it is easy to calculate where a shadow will fall. If the production images have to support a sense of realism then identifying where the source of light is on the set (such as sun, moon or artificial light) will then identify where the shadows will fall. Set models and torches can be helpful in this. When I worked at Boston Opera USA the resident designers (the aforementioned Herbert Senn and Helen Pond) had considerable experience of working with their director and of making the most of the theatre's staging. On the first show I lit with them present I had just finished plotting Act 1, conscious that Herbert had sat behind me very quiet. As I leaned back in my seat to take in the picture Herbert said "Oooh shadows!" I gave him a quizzical look to which he replied: "Your predecessor's mother was frighted by an unlit face!"

Three dimensional scenery will generate shadows and in order that the shadows are not distracting, but follow the logic of the built pieces, the question must be asked: "If this was a real room what effect would the real light source have on the structure?"

New Materials

The traditional materials for scenic construction, such as timber, canvas and fabric have been around literally for centuries but in recent decades these have been joined, or even superseded by metal and plastic derivatives and there have been productions using real water, grass, trees and stone. For the lighting designer meeting these materials on stage for the first time it cannot be assumed that these materials will behave on stage as they appear to do in the outside world. For example, I was once asked to light a drop of water falling from a tree. A substantial amount of experiment was required in order to place the light at the best angle so that the light passing through the drop would refract into the audience. New materials might need more production time. Often new materials appear to have a lot of promise in the showroom but on stage it is important to ask what is the effect of fireproofing? What is the effect on them of heat? Will the material reveal creases?

Dealing with White Sets

White sets present very particular problems for the lighting designer, although they can also present considerable opportunities too. The former arises from the reality that we only see objects because light is reflected into our eyes and white objects will reflect more light than any other surface (such as actors) except a mirror. Thus, if the 'object' is a performer's face set against a white background then there is a risk that the face will appear underlit by comparison with the white background.

Therefore, it is essential that the lighting designer can position the lights in such a way that actor light can be kept off the white surfaces. This depends upon the set providing such angles and access for the light beams and this, in turn, depends on the lighting designer being consulted about these factors before the model (and significantly in these cases the masking) become reality.

I have had a few challenges with white sets which are ingrained in my memory! On one production of 'The Magic Flute' the director wanted the white set lit in white light straight in from the front with the result that the white singers in white costumes simply disappeared. The producer overruled the director and I relit the production – but the director never asked for me again. Once more in Boston on 'Tosca' a sensational black soprano was costumed in black against a dark background and once more disappeared. On this occasion the company had been experimenting with a make-up which reflected light from the star's face so this helped a little. These challenges are usually a fait accompli by the time the lighting designer arrives and the task is firstly to help people understand the laws of physics before the laws of theatre.

Conversely white sets can be provided specifically to act as a bare canvas upon which the lighting designer can paint colours and images. The best example I can recall of this was a white set designed by Marti Flood for the UK tour and West End production of Vanessa Ford and Glyn Robbin's 'The Lion The Witch and the Wardrobe'. I lit Marti's white set in lavender and gentle pink for the bedroom which then crossfaded to blue and white for the snows of Narnia and then crossfaded again to gold and leaf green gobos as Aslan made the snow melt.

Marty Flood's setting for Vanessa Ford's production of 'The Lion The Witch and The Wardrobe' World Premere London (1984). Here the white drapes become a canvas on which to paint colour. The left image is set in a bedroom and the right image set in the snow covered land of Naria reached through the wardrobe in the first scene. Later Aslan melts the snow and the blue is replaced with gold and green dapples. Directed by Richard Williams.

'Tosca' The Opera Company of Boston USA (1986). Directed by Sarah Caldwell. A different challenge from white sets as the soprano, an African American, wore black in this scene and was at risk of disappearing against the black areas of the set, requiring careful backlight to bring her out. Photo by Jim deVeer

Tipping the Mood One Way or the Other

Sometimes it is desirable and effective to adjust the mood of a scene by crossfading from one set of key colours (such as warm tones) to a different one (such as cooler tones) but this often requires a different set of lights for each colour and equally often we simply don't have the equipment available. One way around this is to use neutrals for the main specials (the keylights in photographic terms) so that these will blend in equally well with the range of mood colours you would like to use and provide mood colours, simplistically warms and colds from a few wash lights.

Plotting under these circumstances means gently adding the mood colours to have almost a subliminal effect rather than making the warm or cold highly visible. This technique was described by a major set designer I worked with from the Bolshoi Ballet as "just touch it".

Zoe Atkinson's setting for Perth Theatre Company's production of 'Cox Four' (2002) directed by Alan Becher, in which the pale walls of the box set were gently washed with different colours, changing imperceptibly to underpin the mood of each moment.

Filling in the Holes!

One of the most difficult tasks in lighting design is to provide an even wash across the stage. It's inevitable that the first time the actors come on stage they will find those parts which appear underlit by comparison with the rest. You will, of course, have checked in advance that this isn't so but rest assured the actors will move somewhere you have overlooked! Of course this problem might have resulted from a faulty focus in which case there is an obvious solution but it can also result from a poor balance of intensities. This judgement results from comparing one part of the stage with another and it means that maybe it is better to lower some intensities rather than boost others to achieve evenness.

One Person Shows

I've had the pleasure of lighting several shows performed by one person and in all cases, partially because the artist and I were on tour together, I was able to get to know the artist better than usual.

What I learned from this experience was the degree to which the artist relied on the lighting. I was told that it was even more important that usual to make the artist the most well lit part of the stage so that the audience's attention was less able to wander; after all, the artist could not rely on anyone else on stage for help to keep the audience's interest! Over the length of the tour, or the season, it was possible to work with the artist to tighten the focus for some cues so that the level of contrast between artist and surrounding was greater and more dramatic. Equally they relied on the lighting to help them change mood. In one particular production the actor was very experienced in making films and on television so he was accustomed to being very precise about his positioning.

If lighting positions are critical it helps to show the performer where to stand and this was the lighting designer can also learn what the performer needs to achieve this.

Laptop – Keep it Safe

A lot of contemporary lighting control desks are based on the use of a laptop as the main programming surface. Laptops have other uses of course and left unattended, for example on a production desk in a darkened empty theatre, can be easy prey and if stolen there goes your lighting plot. So, not only do you need to backup the plot anyway but you need to keep that backup somewhere in a safe location.

Record the Hard Patch

Most contemporary lighting controls provide the opportunity to adjust the allocation of control channels to dimmers via the electronic soft patch and such an arrangement will be stored in the plot. But, in any production the dimmers are physically connected to wiring which terminates in the rig and then into a spotlight. If this connection is via a hard plug and socket patch then don't forget to make a record of that hard patch.

Record The Heights of the Lighting Rig

If the production you have designed is intended to tour to other theatres it is critical that you record the positions of the lighting rigging in the initial theatre so that the lighting angles can be accurately reproduced elsewhere. This especially applies to the height of the lighting above the stage, the distance from the bar or pipe to the stage being known as the dead or the trim.

Don't Be So Eager to Help

If you are working as part of a small team there could be times when everyone on stage is lending a hand to clear the stage and change the set. (I have noticed that this rarely applies helping to rig and focus the lights!) However, there is an important point here, by all means lend a hand on stage if you are competent to do so but do not let this erode the time you need as a lighting designer to just sit in the stalls and observe and think. Quiet time is useful too.

Prioritise Jobs List – Critical – Only You Can Tell – Cues

One of the most exciting (and interesting) aspects of theatre is the way productions, initially a kind of organised chaos, quickly start running in some pattern, seemingly all by themselves!

As the production starts coming together on stage it is inevitable that there are lots of jobs yet to finish and equally inevitable that different departments have different priorities, some of which will impact on the lighting design. I have found it helpful to make a list sectioned into priorities, those of the director then the designer, next those critical to the next rehearsal and lower down those which only a lighting designer and the crew will notice. I also use two columns, one for focus notes and one for plotting notes. I find this format helps to almost instantly give a read out of the urgent matters and those which I can delegate to crew or assistants.

Running Cues Without Actors on Stage

It's a reasonable assumption that most of the time a lighting designer's critical task is to make the actors visible. It therefore follows that if you want to run the lighting cues when the stage is available, and more significantly free of actors, then you will not be able to judge the result properly. (However, running cues does provide an opportunity to test fade types and speeds). The level of light for actors can be harsh on some sets so when plotting without the actors on stage, the temptation to lower levels for the sets could prove too strong to resist, but we need to place the actors in an appropriate context.

6 REFLECTIONS

So What Did I Like to Light?

Now that's a very interesting question and I would first have to establish parameters; the Bolshoi Ballet brought me some recognition and respect in the UK, not necessarily abroad, but I wouldn't say it was great lighting – more a logistical feat. Boston Opera likewise brought some respect in USA but it was largely meaningless in the UK. But Boston brought higher fees! Vanessa Ford Productions' Shakespeares and Narnia/Pooh productions brought very enjoyable tours and a daily challenge, on some occasions lighting two shows in one day in two towns! Some other productions stay in my mind for a variety of reasons. Pantomimes for example were fun to work on, especially if the same team and performers were assembled each year, and working in familiar theatres with familiar crew and staying in good and familiar hotels was a lasting pleasure. For lighting however, I would have to say the most recent Spare Parts Puppet Theatre production (The Farmer's Daughter) which brought me the best reviews of my career and which, with Lee Buddle's music, also brought many sheer magic moments which defied analysis.

Matt McVeigh's setting for Spare Parts Puppet Theatre's production of 'The Farmer's Daughter' (2018). Directed by Philip Mitchell. In the left photograph above the soft blue blush is delivered from fresnels pointing at each other across the stage just downstage of the cyc which is thus lit by the spill rather than the main beam. Cycloramas like this need sensitivity, resources, time – and an absence of wrinkles!. (Photos: Simon Pynt)

Balancing the Logistics – The Bolshoi Ballet in a Concert Hall

A lighting design is a mixture of a wide range of definable and indefinable elements and the designer must balance these to be successful. These elements include, in no particular order: ideas, optics, measurements, weights, electrical loads, budgets, schedules and personalities (including his or her own!).

Sometimes a space or a production can pose such a challenge that there is a danger the lighting designer sees the task of resolving the definables more important that resolving the indefinables. In other words the process becomes more important than the result.

This happened to me in 1993 when I was asked to design the lighting for 13 ballets in repertoire for the Bolshoi at London's Royal Albert Hall. This venue, part of the UK's cultural heritage for its regular use for everything from boxing and concerts to military services, seats 8,000 and is effectively a concert hall with a traditional platform in front of which is a large multi-purpose oval space. The Bolshoi's season was, we were told by the RAH staff, the first time the venue had ever been used for one event for such a long season, and this milestone was coupled with the Bolshoi's claim that, in mounting the production on a thrust stage, this was also a first for a classical dance company.

The producer was very experienced at popular music concerts and, correctly judged that there was a large market for the Bolshoi amongst people who would never have gone to the Royal Opera House to see classical ballet but who were familiar with the RAH from its many other guises and, therefore not deterred by it.

I was unknown to the producer but he acquiesced to the Bolshoi's request for my engagement, especially since I had just lit for them in the USA. It quickly became clear that the military precision of the 'rock' touring world was better suited to the task of inserting the 13 ballets into the venue than would perhaps have been the case with a traditional theatre approach. There was seemingly no limit to the resources applied to the task: extensive briefings, drawings and schedules, 24 hour catering, accommodation and transport for all.

From my perspective the producer had indicated that whilst I was not limited by a rental budget nevertheless the season had to run with two staff (the Bolshoi brought their own followspot crew). My experiences with the Bolshoi had taught me that anything could change at anytime and thus I resolved that the rig would deliver any ballet literally at the touch of a switch; there could be no manual refocusing or recolouring.

One anecdote illustrates why. One day the Bolshoi met with the producer and asked to change the sequence of the ballets being performed. The producer patiently explained that this would be impossible because tickets had already been sold. "OK we go home" was the response from the Russians.

Negotiations continued and consequently we only knew what the following day's rehearsals would involve on the day itself.

The solution to the problem of instant access to any ballet, complete with its focus and colour would be easier to solve today with the wide range of (relatively) affordable moving lights but, in 1993 these were not economic in the large quantities I would have needed and, in addition, lacked the subtlety which the Bolshoi required. We did discuss their use but the choreographers were nervous I would move them during the action rather than simply use them in different places and colours in the change-over from one ballet to the next.

(At this point it is worth noting that for a subsequent plan to take this production on tour the Vari*Lite company was extremely helpful in demonstrating models which would have not only been economic but also refined enough for the job. Sadly the tour never took place.)

It has always been my policy to involve my crew in the deliberations about aspects of the rig and it was beneficial on this occasion. I was looking for a colour change system which would cater for the 13 ballets and provide some flexibility for the Bolshoi's tendency for change. Neg Earth, the rental house selected, demonstrated a Morpheus ColorFader which comprised three scrollers, each with one secondary colour but with each frame of the scroll punctured with holes so that, as the holes became bigger with each frame, then the colour would be diluted by the uncoloured light. By mixing darker or lighter secondary colours from each scroll any colour could be created and, the device came complete with a computer already programmed for all the colours in the Lee, Rosco and GamColor ranges. It was possible to vary the selection further by inching each scroll along but it seemed to me that three ranges of colour should be enough for anyone!

The unit contained a fan cooling system and I insisted on a site test with several rigged on a balcony rail just in front of where the public were to sit; the noise was quickly lost in the cavernous volume of the RAH. Eventually I hired every unit in the UK, 76 in all, and placed them on PARS to provide the sidelight usually associated with dance lighting.

I had never worked with ColorFader before but they quickly demonstrated their worth, whatever demands came from the choreographers, we could deliver the colour in a matter of seconds. However, there was one totally unexpected hiccup. Since the majority of the rig was hung in the auditorium itself, serving the thrust stage, it was visible and this was a new experience for the Bolshoi, more accustomed to a proscenium house. Consequently, some choreographers became distracted and wanted to change the colours in the rig to look pretty, ignoring the effect that would result below on the floor and the dancers. This highlighted a fundamental difference in the lighting design which I had tried to explain but clearly failed with at least some key people.

Accustomed to intense side light, virtually parallel to the stage floor, some choreographers did not understand that this was impossible on a thrust stage because of the audience on all three sides, consequently the side light had to come from higher up at the side with the result that more light was visible on the floor than they had ever seen before, and it didn't help that the floorcloth was not evenly painted!

A further problem was only solved when the (Soviet) translator between myself and the choreographers fell ill and was replaced by an English translator. Suddenly the choreographers became more understanding of the difficulties of the new format and this became a turning point – the reason being that the Soviet translator just hadn't wanted to tell the boss something negative, so simply hadn't translated anything.

As the lighting of each ballet went on, and the setup, rehearsal and lighting took over three weeks, I suddenly became conscious that I was relaxing, after all the rig was working, we had solved most of the technical and language problems, and I had achieved a good rapport with the choreographers, designers and my crew.

But I had begun to ignore the main reason I was there, to design the lighting for the public, not to undertake a difficult logistics exercise and then go home.

I think there is always a danger of this, especially in locations which are either not properly equipped theatre spaces and where there is some overarching physical challenge, perhaps outdoors or vast arenas. The lighting designer must be able to address these challenges technically, to know that his or her design can be realised. But the process should never become more important than the result.

Valeri Leventhal's transformation of London's Royal Albert Hall for the Bolshoi Ballet's 13 ballets in repertoire on a vast thrust stage (1993). The candelabra on the proscenium drop were actually painted but I lit them with very tight bullet lights which were the last lights to fade to black and the first to fade in for intervals giving the cue for the rest of the drop and proscenium lights to follow. The painted drop and the built proscenium were lit in different colours which allowed mood changes to underpin the character of the ballet about to be performed.

Matching the Environment – Versailles

For some years in the UK I worked with a company that specialised in operas composed by Frederick Handel, presented with both costumes and instruments authentic to the period. One performance was staged in the small theatre in the Palace of Versailles near Paris in which the set comprised wings and borders painted in the perspective style of the period. Initially I plotted the lighting using my preferred 'high-side' or 'end pipe' side light which brought out the texture of the very full costumes and provided a crispness separating the performers from the backdrops. But something was wrong, the images were out of place with the setting. Too modern, I thought and then set about relighting by reducing the intensity of the side light and pushing up high the theatre's inbuilt footlights.

Technically this 'look' would probably not have worked anywhere else but in an authentic 18th Century setting it was correct.

The author's photograph of the Bolshoi Theatre in Moscow with the set for the opera 'The Balcony' showing trucks in place. At this time the Bolshoi was not used to operating scene changes in view and the trucks caused much discussion (1990).

Less Successful

Not all productions are successes; overall a judgement that can be measured at least critically, publicly, financially, visually and/or technically. In lighting terms there can be as many ways of assessment too. Was the client satisfied? Did the execution of the design support the artists and the work?

Was the design realised on time and on budget? Did it meet your own criteria? Each member of the creative team has varying degrees of control over the mechanisms that relate to these criteria and few will be exercised in a way that results in total success or failure. Some degree of post-portem, either personally or collectively, should help to avoid the repetition of any pitfalls that were encountered.

Some years ago I was asked to go to the (then) Soviet Union as part of a United States cultural party, returning the complement of the Soviet

Union's cultural visit to Boston USA for which I was lighting consultant and which required me and my team to address several productions across a range of venues. The idea was the brainchild of Boston Opera's Sarah Caldwell and the détente preceded that then being courted between leaders Reagan and Gorbechev who later allegedly tried to claim the Festival as an example of the success of their discussions!

The production in question was 'The Balcony', an opera based on the Genet play. The piece was being designed and rehearsed in the United States but sadly the company could not afford for me to travel from London to see the rehearsals, added to which the libretto was not available and only part of the music so I had little to go on except drawings of the set. The production manager and I made a recce to Moscow to assess the venue, the famed Bolshoi Theatre.

We stood quietly at the side of the vast stage, a 25m wide proscenium, lighting bars 12m out, and tried to gauge how our respective disciplines would fare. In my case rigging extra equipment or making changes to the standard rig was not within the scope of the company's contract so the standard rig had to suffice.

When I arrived for the actual production the set construction was underway, this had been built in the USA and shipped across but some miscommunication meant that alterations were necessary. This was beginning to take longer than expected because at that point the Bolshoi lacked power tools and thinking the set was finished the US crew had only brought a few with them.

The set was a vast three storey, three sided gallery of louvred windows in off-white coupled with a series of insets on wagons.

Most of the standing lighting rig was provided with motorised pan and tilt although I soon discovered that the combination of the high 12m trim and the mechanisms meant that in reality little variation from straight down was feasible. The exception to this was a pair of beamlights on the ends of the bars which could sweep in any direction and which thus became my 'specials' for highlighting key parts of the set or the action.

The crew also permitted some lighting equipment to be rigged in the wings to backlight the louvred windows.

Whilst the crew could not have been more helpful we learned that the daytime crew were purely for rigging and did not work the shows, leaving at 4pm when the show crew arrived. Thus technical rehearsals before

4pm were of limited use because the cues would actually be operated by someone else. A further complication arose from the fact that the wagons and other set paraphernalia were to be moved in view of the audience and at this point we were told that the Bolshoi didn't do this because set changes were always done behind the house curtain. Consequently set changes took longer to arrange because new techniques had to be translated and learned.

A final complication was that when the stage was not being used for construction, alteration or technical work it was colonised by the choreographer who otherwise had nowhere to rehearse. So lighting time, on a darkened stage, was non-existent.

Somewhere in all this I was trying to learn the plot and the music, my busy director's requirements (she was also conducting the orchestra) and attempting to produce anything that resembled a design.

The dress rehearsal loomed before us and, since we hadn't been able to light the show or undertake a technical, we tried to postpone it. However, the public had been invited and consequently it went ahead. I had decided to work the board and try to light over the dress. What the public thought we never knew but the combination of the contemporary score and frequent technical hitches (often accompanied by a stalled orchestra and visible on-stage technical discussions) must have made for a very strange evening.

I missed several cues either because I had no idea what was happening or mishearing the stage manager, or both.

A dejected team met afterwards to discuss the next day's work. I explained my plan for a quiet morning lighting session and did make what I thought were significant improvements informed by my knowledge of the first ever (albeit haphazard) rehearsal the night before. My spirits were sustained by sympathetic set designers but my director never spoke to me again.

Whilst this story doesn't contain much about actual lighting it nevertheless lays out some of the factors which can influence it (and of course the same goes for any other production department).

Whilst the reader might feel some of the situations resulted from poor production management, I would submit that there are issues of complexity and gravity that are beyond a production manager to control. Much of what happened at the Bolshoi was the result of a gigantic learning process slowed considerably by language differences. In retrospect I think I fell into the same trap as everyone else, a mindset that things couldn't get worse, would therefore get better tomorrow, and thus there would be time to apply our normal approach and produce results.

My approach overall is a pragmatic one, I might gently challenge the resources I have to work with but overall I'm more likely to work within them than not. I like to study the 'givens' as soon as possible, the script, the set, the venue, the equipment. I like to take time to draw the set into the venue in plan and section – this is usually a voyage of discovery because many plans contain inaccuracies.

Consequently, if I perceive that a particular problem might arise then I will make a plan to address it. In lighting terms this might mean: if access is the problem then working within existing positions and not rigging new ones, if plotting time is scarce then establishing basic states and perfecting those before adding any more, if equipment is scarce then prioritising a good general cover and reserving a handful of instruments for just a few effective specials.

Once in the theatre, basic focus and states established – a foundation – I like to move quickly through focusing to experimenting with a few key states so that I know as soon as possible what works and what doesn't. My target for delivering a finished product is the first night not the technical rehearsal so I'm refining focusing and plotting throughout the technical and early dresses.

However, the difficulty for all of us on this production was that we didn't know what we didn't know so contingency plans couldn't be made.

Is it Going to Get Any Better?

Many years ago I was asked to light a Handel Opera at the Royal Opera House in Covent Garden in London. The production was not mounted by the Opera House itself but by a small opera company which was to take the production on to Italy. The demands of the intimate Italian houses dictated that the set would be small and the demands of the budget dictated that we only had one day to rig the set, focus, plot, rehearse and perform in London.

Fortunately the rigid schedules of the Opera House decided our production schedule for us and equally fortunately the Opera House crew were very experienced and couldn't have been more helpful to this slightly astonished lighting designer who couldn't quite believe he was actually lighting on the revered stage.

The good points ended there. We weren't allowed to refocus or recolour the front of house (because of the repertoire system) and the small set meant that the stage rig (which we could refocus and recolour) was so far offstage and above the set that getting any light in to the correct places was difficult and time consuming. As we had been warned, the orchestra would stop in mid note if the rehearsal was due to end, and that is exactly what happened so we never heard or saw the last act!

As the house manager hovered nervously around the production desk anxiously looking at his watch and waiting to open the house, I was still plotting. At this precise moment there was a power failure in the stalls and the production desk (resembling a scene from a space control panel) went to darkness.

As the ushers started taking up positions electricians were crawling around my feet and a managed to get something on the plot. It was at this point that the producer, my client, asked: "Is it going to get any better?" I didn't answer but thought it could hardly get any worse! I never made it to Italy and my mentor Francis Reid had that pleasure. These situations are hard to correct whilst they are happening and the best you can do is try and keep calm, help your colleagues, and deliver a result that will still keep the audience in their seats!

A Golden Memory – Anthony Newley

Mr Newley was a significant singer, actor and composer with a long list of hits and musicals to his name (many the result of collaborations with other notables). For a brief period in the 1990s in the UK I was lighting designer to Mr Newley for his cabaret performances in London's West End and on tour. At the time I met him he had returned from the US having appeared in cabaret in Las Vegas. I was slightly apprehensive and curious to see if his Vegas experiences had increased his expectations of what a lighting designer could do. I needn't have worried, at all times he was a pleasure to be with, open to ideas and always totally professional.

Mr Newley arranged a run-through for me of his act, so there I was in a rehearsal room, just me Mr Newley and his pianist and he performed the hour long set just for me. We talked about how he saw the different songs being presented, not so much in lighting terms as how important they had been to his life. For my part I began to suggest themes of colours to enhance the character of the different emotions. He was very supportive of this and agreed to try this out. I was slightly puzzled that this did not seem to have been a feature of his act before.

The first performance was on tour out of London and for this (and all subsequent performances) I operated the lighting desk. This enabled me to respond instantly to the emotion of the moment as Mr Newley in turn responded to his audience. Music, lighting, enjoyment. Heaven!

Did I Like All the Productions I Lit?

I've had the good fortune to light over 500 productions in the USA, UK and Australia and despite keeping reasonably accurate archives the lighting design of some productions I cannot recall. I might however recall some productions for other reasons such as personalities, locations or performances and this maybe illustrates the reality that sometimes the production simply does not offer opportunities for work to be noticed and that's as it should be surely? Sometimes I have accepted work because I enjoyed working with the director, or the design was especially interesting, but, sometimes the play was depressing and so I just focused on bringing out the key elements of the director's clarifications. It depends I think on your own journey and tastes. I will always enjoy something with music, even though I can't read a note or play an instrument, and I will always enjoy Shakespeare because I'm always moved by the effect words have that were written over 400 years ago. For me the key is always whether the piece uses theatre and celebrates the theatrical, a live experience unique every night, and to be part of that *is* memorable.

The reality is that not everything you light will be significant; take pleasure in a good portfolio and paying the rent!

Rachel Arianne Ogle in Spare Parts Puppet Theatre's production of 'The Fox' (2015). Directed by Michael Barlow. This was an inspiring collaboration of puppetry, costume, dance, music, and projection. (Photo: Simon Pynt)

THE TEN COMMANDMENTS

- Thou shalt leave the theatre at regular intervals to partake of food, liquid refreshment and sleep and especially to rest thine eyes.
- Thou shall not place a lighting instrument in the rig without a clear idea of its purpose.
- Thou shalt be able to explain where a hole would appear if the instrument's bulb shall blow.
- Thou shalt not be tempted to light the scenery at the expense of the actors.
- Thou shalt not treat the production schedule or the budget as a graven image but shall continually work to make the best use of available resources for all the team.
- Thou shalt not worship the process at the expense of the outcome.
- Thou shalt never forget thine audience.
- Thou shalt not forget that a lighting state cannot be judged until it is cued in the correct place.
- Thou shalt not delete an effect because it defies objective assessment; lighting design is a creative process which can defy analysis.
- Thou shalt give thanks for working in some beautiful buildings with beautiful words and music, much of which was first conceived decades ago, and, for being able to contribute to more valuable work. And for being paid for all this!

The cauldron scene from Vanessa Ford Production's 'Macbeth'. Lights were concealed in the cauldron to shoot up and overhead there were matching downlights creating a pillar of light into which witches and mortals could play.

ENTERTAINMENT TECHNOLOGY PRESS

FREE SUBSCRIPTION SERVICE

Keeping Up To Date with

On Being a Lighting Designer

Entertainment Technology titles are continually up-dated, and all major changes and additions are listed in date order in the relevant dedicated area of the publisher's website. Simply go to the front page of www.etnow.com and click on the BOOKS button. From there you can locate the title and be connected through to the latest information and services related to the publication.

The author of the title welcomes comments and suggestions about the book and can be contacted by email at: graham2@iinet.net.au

Titles Published by Entertainment Technology Press

50 Rigging Calls *Chris Higgs, Cristiano Giavedoni 246pp* **£16.95**
ISBN: 9781904031758
Chris Higgs, author of ETP's two leading titles on rigging, An Introduction to Rigging in the Entertainment Industry and Rigging for Entertainment: Regulations and Practice, has collected together 50 articles he has provided regularly for Lighting + Sound International magazine from 2005 to date. They provide a wealth of information for those practising the craft within the entertainment technology industry. The book is profusely illustrated with caricature drawings by Christiano Giavedoni, featuring the popular rigging expert Mario.

ABC of Theatre Jargon *Francis Reid 106pp* **£9.95** ISBN: 9781904031093
This glossary of theatrical terminology explains the common words and phrases that are used in normal conversation between actors, directors, designers, technicians and managers.

Aluminium Structures in the Entertainment Industry *Peter Hind 234pp* **£24.95**
ISBN: 9781904031062
Aluminium Structures in the Entertainment Industry aims to educate the reader in all aspects of the design and safe usage of temporary and permanent aluminium structures specific to the entertainment industry – such as roof structures, PA towers, temporary staging, etc.

AutoCAD – A Handbook for Theatre Users 4th ed *David Ripley 318pp* **£32.00**
ISBN: 9781904031901
From 'Setting Up' to 'Drawing in Three Dimensions' via 'Drawings Within Drawings', this compact and fully illustrated guide to AutoCAD covers everything from the basics to full colour rendering and remote 3D plotting. Fourth, completely revised edition, March 2018.

Automation in the Entertainment Industry – A User's Guide *Mark Ager and John Hastie 382pp* **£29.95** ISBN: 9781904031581
In the last 15 years, there has been a massive growth in the use of automation in entertainment, especially in theatres, and it is now recognised as its own discipline. However, it is still only used in around 5% of theatres worldwide. In the next 25 years, given current growth patterns, that figure will rise to 30%. This will mean that the majority of theatre personnel, including directors, designers, technical staff, actors and theatre management, will come into contact with automation for the first time at some point in their careers. This book is intended to provide insights and practical advice from those who use automation, to help the first-time user understand the issues and avoid the pitfalls in its implementation.

Basics – A Beginner's Guide to Lighting Design *Peter Coleman 92pp* **£9.95**
ISBN: 9781904031413
The fourth in the author's 'Basics' series, this title covers the subject area in four main sections: The Concept, Practical Matters, Related Issues and The Design Into Practice. In an area that is difficult to be definitive, there are several things that cross all the boundaries of all lighting design and it's these areas that the author seeks to help with.

Basics – A Beginner's Guide to Special Effects *Peter Coleman 82pp* **£9.95**
ISBN: 9781904031338
This title introduces newcomers to the world of special effects. It describes all types of special effects including pyrotechnic, smoke and lighting effects, projections, noise machines, etc. It places emphasis on the safe storage, handling and use of pyrotechnics.

Basics – A Beginner's Guide to Stage Lighting *Peter Coleman 86pp* **£9.95**
ISBN: 9781904031208
This title does what it says: it introduces newcomers to the world of stage lighting. It will not teach the reader the art of lighting design, but will teach beginners much about the 'nuts and bolts' of stage lighting.

Basics – A Beginner's Guide to Stage Sound *Peter Coleman 86pp* **£9.95**
ISBN: 9781904031277
This title does what it says: it introduces newcomers to the world of stage sound. It will not teach the reader the art of sound design, but will teach beginners much about the background to sound reproduction in a theatrical environment.

Basics: A Beginner's Guide to Stage Management *Peter Coleman 64pp* **£7.95**
ISBN: 9781904031475
The fifth in Peter Coleman's popular 'Basics' series, this title provides a practical insight into, and the definition of, the role of stage management. Further chapters describe Cueing or 'Calling' the Show (the Prompt Book), and the Hardware and Training for Stage Management. This is a book about people and systems, without which most of the technical equipment used by others in the performance workplace couldn't function.

Building Better Theaters *Michael Mell 180pp* **£16.95** ISBN: 9781904031406
A title within our Consultancy Series, this book describes the process of designing a theatre, from the initial decision to build through to opening night. Michael Mell's book provides a step-by-step guide to the design and construction of performing arts facilities. Chapters discuss: assembling your team, selecting an architect, different construction methods, the architectural design process, construction of the theatre, theatrical systems and equipment, the stage, backstage, the auditorium, ADA requirements and the lobby. Each chapter clearly describes what to expect and how to avoid surprises. It is a must-read for architects, planners, performing arts groups, educators and anyone who may be considering building or renovating a theatre.

Carry on Fading *Francis Reid 216pp* **£20.00** ISBN: 9781904031642
This is a record of five of the best years of the author's life. Years so good that the only downside is the pangs of guilt at enjoying such contentment in a world full of misery induced by greed, envy and imposed ideologies. Fortunately Francis' DNA is high on luck, optimism and blessing counting.

Case Studies in Crowd Management
Chris Kemp, Iain Hill, Mick Upton, Mark Hamilton 206pp **£16.95**
ISBN: 9781904031482
This important work has been compiled from a series of research projects carried out by the staff of the Centre for Crowd Management and Security Studies at Buckinghamshire Chilterns University College (now Bucks New University), and seminar work carried out in Berlin and Groningen with partner Yourope. It includes case studies, reports and a crowd management safety plan for a major outdoor rock concert, safe management of rock concerts utilising a triple barrier safety system and pan-European Health & Safety Issues.

Case Studies in Crowd Management, Security and Business Continuity
Chris Kemp, Patrick Smith 274pp **£24.95** ISBN: 9781904031635
The creation of good case studies to support work in progress and to give answers to those seeking guidance in their quest to come to terms with perennial questions is no easy task. The first Case Studies in Crowd Management book focused mainly on a series of festivals and events that had a number of issues which required solving. This book focuses on a series of events that had major issues that impacted on the every day delivery of the events researched.

Charles John Phipps F.S.A. Architect to the Victorian Theatre
Görel Garlick 402pp **£25.95** ISBN: 9781904031895
This book is the first in-depth biography of the leading Victorian theatre architect Charles Phipps. His designs dislodged the Victorian theatre from its dependence on the Georgian playhouse and ushered in a new modernity utilising the latest technology in lighting, stage machinery and building construction and his work was a major influence on younger architects, notably Frank Matcham. The book traces Phipps's colourful career and his, often fraught, relationships with clients, as well as his attitude to changing safety regulations and those who attempted to enforce them. The book also re-examines the Exeter Theatre fire and its aftermath, which reverberated throughout the country, and how Phipps managed to cling on to his career before returning with new ideas in his last years.

Close Protection – The Softer Skills *Geoffrey Padgham* 132pp **£11.95**
ISBN: 9781904031390
This is the first educational book in a new 'Security Series' for Entertainment Technology Press, and it coincides with the launch of the new 'Protective Security Management' Foundation Degree at Buckinghamshire Chilterns University College (now Bucks New University). The author is a former full-career Metropolitan Police Inspector from New Scotland Yard with 27 years' experience of close protection (CP). For 22 of those years he specialised in operations and senior management duties with the Royalty Protection Department at Buckingham Palace, followed by five years in the private security industry specialising in CP training design and delivery. His wealth of protection experience comes across throughout the text, which incorporates sound advice and exceptional practical guidance, subtly separating fact from fiction. This publication is an excellent form of reference material for experienced operatives, students and trainees.

A Comparative Study of Crowd Behaviour at Two Major Music Events
Chris Kemp, Iain Hill, Mick Upton 78pp **£7.95**   ISBN: 9781904031253
A compilation of the findings of reports made at two major live music concerts, and in particular crowd behaviour, which is followed from ingress to egress.

Control Freak *Wayne Howell 270pp* **£28.95**   ISBN: 9781904031550
Control Freak is the second book by Wayne Howell. It provides an in depth study of DMX512 and the new RDM (Remote Device Management) standards. The book is aimed at both users and developers and provides a wealth of real world information based on the author's twenty year experience of lighting control.

Copenhagen Opera House   *Richard Brett and John Offord 272pp* **£32.00**
ISBN: 9781904031420
Completed in a little over three years, the Copenhagen Opera House opened with a royal gala performance on 15th January 2005. Built on a spacious brown-field site, the building is a landmark venue and this book provides the complete technical background story to an opera house set to become a benchmark for future design and planning. Sixteen chapters by relevant experts involved with the project cover everything from the planning of the auditorium and studio stage, the stage engineering, stage lighting and control and architectural lighting through to acoustic design and sound technology plus technical summaries.

Corporate Event Production – Effective, face-to-face, corporate communication or Reaching 'The guy at the back, with bad eyesight - who'd rather be in the bar'
David Clement 324pp **£29.95**   ISBN: 9781904031840
A real-world insight into a specific industry sector: Corporate Event Production – the business of face-to-face communication. What it actually feels like to work in live events. The subtitle of 'Reaching the guy at the back with bad eyesight – who'd rather be in the bar' encapsulates the producer's challenge of creating an equally memorable experience for all attendees.
Structured around the project timeline – from receipt of a brief, to creative response and pitching, through pre-production design and planning to creating and directing the show on the day – the book is full of industry anecdotes, over 160 reference images, useful tips and guidelines. The stage-by-stage process of designing an engaging and truly effective live event.

Cue 80 *Francis Reid 310pp* **£17.95**   ISBN: 9781904031659
Although Francis Reid's work in theatre has been visual rather than verbal, writing has provided crucial support. Putting words on paper has been the way in which he organised and clarified his thoughts. And in his self-confessed absence of drawing skills, writing has helped him find words to communicate his visual thinking in discussions with the rest of the creative team. As a by-product, this process of searching for the right words to help formulate and analyse ideas has resulted in half-a-century of articles in theatre journals. Cue 80 is an anthology of these articles and is released in celebration of Francis' 80th birthday.

The DMX 512-A Handbook – Design and Implementation of DMX Enabled Products and Networks *James Eade 150pp* **£13.95** ISBN: 9781904031727
This guidebook was originally conceived as a guide to the new DMX512-A standard on behalf of the ESTA Controls Protocols Working Group (CPWG). It has subsequently been updated and is aimed at all levels of reader from technicians working with or servicing equipment in the field as well as manufacturers looking to build in DMX control to their lighting products. It also gives thorough guidance to consultants and designers looking to design DMX networks.

Electric Shadows: an Introduction to Video and Projection on Stage *Nick Moran 234pp* **£23.95** ISBN: 9781904031734
Electric Shadows aims to guide the emerging video designer through the many simple and difficult technical and aesthetic choices and decisions he or she has to make in taking their design from outline idea through to realisation. The main body of the book takes the reader through the process of deciding what content will be projected onto what screen or screens to make the best overall production design. The book will help you make electric shadows that capture the attention of your audience, to help you tell your stories in just the way you want.

Electrical Safety for Live Events *Marco van Beek 98pp* **£16.95** ISBN: 9781904031284
This title covers electrical safety regulations and good practise pertinent to the entertainment industries and includes some basic electrical theory as well as clarifying the "do's and don't's" of working with electricity.

Entertainment Electronics *Anton Woodward 154pp* **£15.95** ISBN: 9781904031819
Electronic engineering in theatres has become quite prevalent in recent years, whether for lighting, sound, automation or props – so it has become an increasingly important skill for the theatre technician to possess. This book is intended to give the theatre technician a good grasp of the fundamental principles of electronics without getting too bogged down with maths so that many of the mysteries of electronics are revealed.

Entertainment in Production Volume 1: 1994-1999 *Rob Halliday 254pp* **£24.95** ISBN: 9781904031512
Entertainment in Production Volume 2: 2000-2006 *Rob Halliday 242poo* £24.95 ISBN: 9781904031529
Rob Halliday has a dual career as a lighting designer/programmer and author and in these two volumes he provides the intriguing but comprehensive technical background stories behind the major musical productions and other notable projects spanning the period 1994 to 2005. Having been closely involved with the majority of the events described, the author is able to present a first-hand and all-encompassing portrayal of how many of the major shows across the past decade came into being. From *Oliver!* and *Miss Saigon* to *Mamma Mia!* and *Mary Poppins*, here the complete technical story unfolds. The books, which are profusely illustrated, are in large part an adapted selection of articles that first appeared in the magazine *Lighting&Sound International*.

Entertainment Technology Yearbook 2008 *John Offord 220pp* **£14.95**
ISBN: 9781904031543
The Entertainment Technology Yearbook 2008 covers the year 2007 and includes picture coverage of major industry exhibitions in Europe compiled from the pages of Entertainment Technology magazine and the etnow.com website, plus articles and pictures of production, equipment and project highlights of the year.

The Exeter Theatre Fire *David Anderson 202pp*   **£24.95** ISBN: 9781904031130
This title is a fascinating insight into the events that led up to the disaster at the Theatre Royal, Exeter, on the night of September 5th 1887. The book details what went wrong, and the lessons that were learned from the event.

Fading into Retirement *Francis Reid 124pp* **£17.95** ISBN: 9781904031352
This is the final book in Francis Reid's fading trilogy which, with Fading Light and Carry on Fading, updates the Hearing the Light record of places visited, performances seen, and people met. Never say never, but the author uses the 'final' label because decreasing mobility means that his ability to travel is diminished to the point that his life is now contained within a very few square miles. His memories are triggered by over 600 CDs, half of them Handel and 100 or so DVDs supplemented by a rental subscription to LOVEFiLM.

Fading Light – A Year in Retirement *Francis Reid 136pp* **£14.95**
ISBN: 9781904031352
Francis Reid, the lighting industry's favourite author, describes a full year in retirement. "Old age is much more fun than I expected," he says. Fading Light describes visits and experiences to the author's favourite theatres and opera houses, places of relaxation and re-visits to scholarly institutions.

Focus on Lighting Technology *Richard Cadena 120pp* **£17.95** ISBN: 9781904031147
This concise work unravels the mechanics behind modern performance lighting and appeals to designers and technicians alike. Packed with clear, easy-to-read diagrams, the book provides excellent explanations behind the technology of performance lighting.

The Followspot Guide *Nick Mobsby 450pp* **£28.95** ISBN: 9781904031499
The first in ETP's Equipment Series, Nick Mobsby's Followspot Guide tells you everything you need to know about followspots, from their history through to maintenance and usage. Its pages include a technical specification of 193 followspots from historical to the latest versions from major manufacturers.

From Ancient Rome to Rock 'n' Roll – a Review of the UK Leisure Security Industry *Mick Upton 198pp* **£14.95** ISBN: 9781904031505
From stewarding, close protection and crowd management through to his engagement as a senior consultant Mick Upton has been ever present in the events industry. A founder of ShowSec International in 1982 he was its chairman until 2000. The author has led the way on training within the sector. He set up the ShowSec Training Centre and has acted as

a consultant at the Bramshill Police College. He has been prominent in the development of courses at Buckinghamshire New University where he was awarded a Doctorate in 2005. Mick has received numerous industry awards. His book is a personal account of the development and professionalism of the sector across the past 50 years.

Gobos for Image Projection   *Michael Hall and Julie Harper 176pp*   **£25.95**
ISBN: 9781904031628
In this first published book dedicated totally to the gobo, the authors take the reader through from the history of projection to the development of the present day gobo. And there is broad practical advice and ample reference information to back it up. A feature of the work is the inclusion, interspersed throughout the text, of comment and personal experience in the use and application of gobos from over 25 leading lighting designers worldwide.

Health and Safety Aspects in the Live Music Industry   *Chris Kemp, Iain Hill 300pp*
£30.00   ISBN: 9781904031222
This major work includes chapters on various safety aspects of live event production and is written by specialists in their particular areas of expertise.

Health and Safety in the Live Music and Event Technical Produciton Industry
Chris Hannam   74pp   **£12.95**   ISBN: 9781904031802
This book covers the real basics of health and safety in the live music and event production industry in a simple jargon free manner that can also be used as the perfect student course note accompaniment to the various safety passport schemes that now exist in our industry.

Health and Safety Management for Tour and Production Managers and
Self-Employment in the Live Music and Events Industry
Chris Hannam   136pp   **£11.95**   ISBN: 9781904031864
Two books in one: **Health and Safety Management for Tour and Production Managers** is designed to give simple, basic health and safety information to bands, artists, tour, stage and production managers, crew chiefs, heads of department, supervisors or line managers and has been designed as a follow on from *Health And Safety in the Live Music and Event Technical Production Industry*. It will also be of use to local crew companies, especially their crew chiefs and managers.
The second book is **Self-Employment in the Live Music and Events Industry**
A Guide for the Self-Employed and those who use the services of the Self-Employed

Health and Safety Management in the Live Music and Events Industry   *Chris Hannam 1164pp*   **£45.00**   ISBN: 9781904031918
This title covers the health and safety regulations and their application regarding all aspects of staging live entertainment events, and is an invaluable manual for production managers and event organisers. Completely revised and updated February 2018.

Hearing the Light – 50 Years Backstage *Francis Reid 280pp* **£24.95**
ISBN: 9781904031185
This highly enjoyable memoir delves deeply into the theatricality of the industry. The author's almost fanatical interest in opera, his formative period as lighting designer at Glyndebourne and his experiences as a theatre administrator, writer and teacher make for a broad and unique background.

Introduction to Live Sound *Roland Higham 174pp* **£16.95**
ISBN: 9781904031796
This new title aims to provide working engineers and newcomers alike with a concise knowledge base that explains some of the theory and principles that they will encounter every day. It should provide for the student and newcomer to the field a valuable compendium of helpful knowledge.

An Introduction to Rigging in the Entertainment Industry *Chris Higgs 272pp* **£24.95**
ISBN: 9781904031123
This title is a practical guide to rigging techniques and practices and also thoroughly covers safety issues and discusses the implications of working within recommended guidelines and regulations. Second edition revised September 2008.

Let There be Light – Entertainment Lighting Software Pioneers in Conversation
Robert Bell 390pp **£32.00**   ISBN: 9781904031246
Robert Bell interviews a distinguished group of software engineers working on entertainment lighting ideas and products.

Light and Colour Filters *Michael Hall and Eddie Ruffell 286pp* **£23.95**
ISBN: 9781904031598
Written by two acknowledged and respected experts in the field, this book is destined to become the standard reference work on the subject. The title chronicles the development and use of colour filters and also describes how colour is perceived and how filters function. Up-to-date reference tables will help the practitioner make better and more specific choices of colour.

Lighting for Roméo and Juliette *John Offord 172pp* **£26.95**   ISBN: 9781904031161
John Offord describes the making of the Vienna State Opera production from the lighting designer's viewpoint – from the point where director Jürgen Flimm made his decision not to use scenery or sets and simply employ the expertise of lighting designer Patrick Woodroffe.

Lighting Systems for TV Studios *Nick Mobsby 570pp* **£45.00**   ISBN: 9781904031000
Lighting Systems for TV Studios, now in its second edition, is the first book specifically written on the subject and has become the 'standard' resource work for studio planning and design covering the key elements of system design, luminaires, dimming, control, data networks and suspension systems as well as detailing the infrastructure items such as cyclorama, electrical and ventilation. TV lighting principles are explained and some history on TV broadcasting, camera technology and the equipment is provided to help set the scene!

The second edition includes applications for sine wave and distributed dimming, moving lights, Ethernet and new cool lamp technology.

Lighting Techniques for Theatre-in-the-Round *Jackie Staines 188pp* **£24.95**
ISBN: 9781904031017
Lighting Techniques for Theatre-in-the-Round is a unique reference source for those working on lighting design for theatre-in-the-round for the first time. It is the first title to be published specifically on the subject and it also provides some anecdotes and ideas for more challenging shows, and attempts to blow away some of the myths surrounding lighting in this format.

Lighting the Diamond Jubilee Concert *Durham Marenghi 102pp* **£19.95**
ISBN: 9781904031673
In this highly personal landmark document the show's lighting designer Durham Marenghi pays tribute to the team of industry experts who each played an important role in bringing the Diamond Jubilee Concert to fruition, both for television and live audiences. The book contains colour production photography throughout and describes the production processes and the thinking behind them. In his Foreword, BBC Executive Producer Guy Freeman states: "Working with the whole lighting team on such a special project was a real treat for me and a fantastic achievement for them, which the pages of this book give a remarkable insight into."

Lighting the Stage *Francis Reid 120pp* **£14.95** ISBN: 9781904031086
Lighting the Stage discusses the human relationships involved in lighting design – both between people, and between these people and technology. The book is written from a highly personal viewpoint and its 'thinking aloud' approach is one that Francis Reid has used in his writings over the past 30 years.

Miscellany of Lighting and Stagecraft *Michael Hall & Julie Harper 222pp* **£22.95**
ISBN: 9781904031680
This title will help schools, colleges, amateurs, technicians and all those interested in practical theatre and performance to understand, in an entertaining and informative way, the key backstage skills. Within its pages, numerous professionals share their own special knowledge and expertise, interspersed with diversions of historic interest and anecdotes from those practising at the front line of the industry. As a result, much of the advice and skills set out have not previously been set in print. The editors' intention with this book is to provide a Miscellany that is not ordered or categorised in strict fashion, but rather encourages the reader to flick through or dip into it, finding nuggets of information and anecdotes to entertain, inspire and engender curiosity – also to invite further research or exploration and generally encourage people to enter the industry and find out for themselves.

Mr Phipps' Theatre *Mark Jones, John Pick 172pp* £17.95 ISBN: 9781904031383
Mark Jones and John Pick describe "The Sensational Story of Eastbourne's Royal Hippodrome" – formerly Eastbourne Theatre Royal. An intriguing narrative, the book sets

the story against a unique social history of the town. Peter Longman, former director of The Theatres Trust, provides the Foreword.

The National Theatre: A Place for Plays *ABTT 130pp* **£11.95** ISBN: 9781904031932
Paule Constable and Richard Pilbrow hosted a one-day Symposium on 30th October 2016 to celebrate the 40th Anniversary of the opening by Her Majesty the Queen of the National Theatre designed by Sir Denys Lasdun. The National Theatre: A Place for Plays, presented by the Association of British Theatre Technicians in association with the National Theatre, was about Theatre and Architecture: a discussion, a confrontation, a misunderstanding or a collaboration?

Northen Lights *Michael Northen 256pp* **£17.95** ISBN: 9781904031666
Many books have been written by famous personalities in the theatre about their lives and work. However this is probably one of the first memoirs by someone who has spent his entire career behind scenes, and not in front of the footlights. As a lighting designer and as consultant to designers and directors, Michael Northen worked through an exciting period of fifty years of theatrical history from the late nineteen thirties in theatres in the UK and abroad, and on productions ranging from Shakespeare, opera and ballet to straight plays, pantomimes and cabaret. This is not a complicated technical text book, but is intended to give an insight into some of the 300 productions in which he had been involved and some of the directors, the designers and backstage staff he have worked with, viewed from a new angle.

Pages From Stages *Anthony Field 204pp* **£17.95** ISBN: 9781904031260
Anthony Field explores the changing style of theatres including interior design, exterior design, ticket and seat prices, and levels of service, while questioning whether the theatre still exists as a place of entertainment for regular theatre-goers.

People, Places, Performances *Remembered by Francis Reid 60pp* **£8.95**
ISBN: 9781904031765
In growing older, the Author has found that memories, rather than featuring the events, increasingly tend to focus on the people who caused them, the places where they happened and the performances that arose. So Francis Reid has used these categories in endeavouring to compile a brief history of the second half of the twentieth century.

Practical Dimming *Nick Mobsby 364pp* **£22.95** ISBN: 97819040313444
This important and easy to read title covers the history of electrical and electronic dimming, how dimmers work, current dimmer types from around the world, planning of a dimming system, looking at new sine wave dimming technology and distributed dimming. Integration of dimming into different performance venues as well as the necessary supporting electrical systems are fully detailed. Significant levels of information are provided on the many different forms and costs of potential solutions as well as how to plan specific solutions. Architectural dimming for the likes of hotels, museums and shopping centres is included. Practical Dimming is a companion book to Practical DMX and is designed for all involved in the use, operation and design of dimming systems.

Practical DMX *Nick Mobsby 276pp* **£16.95** ISBN: 9781904031369
In this highly topical and important title the author details the principles of DMX, how to plan a network, how to choose equipment and cables, with data on products from around the world, and how to install DMX networks for shows and on a permanently installed basis. The easy style of the book and the helpful fault finding tips, together with a review of different DMX testing devices provide an ideal companion for all lighting technicians and system designers. An introduction to Ethernet and Canbus networks are provided as well as tips on analogue networks and protocol conversion. It also includes a chapter on Remote Device Management.

A Practical Guide to Health and Safety in the Entertainment Industry
Marco van Beek 120pp **£14.95** ISBN: 9781904031048
This book is designed to provide a practical approach to Health and Safety within the Live Entertainment and Event industry. It gives industry-pertinent examples, and seeks to break down the myths surrounding Health and Safety.

Production Management *Joe Aveline 134pp* **£17.95** ISBN: 9781904031109
Joe Aveline's book is an in-depth guide to the role of the Production Manager, and includes real-life practical examples and 'Aveline's Fables' – anecdotes of his experiences with real messages behind them.

Rigging for Entertainment: Regulations and Practice *Chris Higgs 156pp* **£19.95**
ISBN: 9781904031215
Continuing where he left off with his highly successful An Introduction to Rigging in the Entertainment Industry, Chris Higgs' second title covers the regulations and use of equipment in greater detail.

Rock Solid Ethernet *Wayne Howell 304pp* **£23.95** ISBN: 9781904031697
Now in its third completely revised and reset edition, Rock Solid Ethernet is aimed specifically at specifiers, installers and users of entertainment industry systems, and will give the reader a thorough grounding in all aspects of computer networks, whatever industry they may work in. The inclusion of historical and technical 'sidebars' make for an enjoyable as well as an informative read.

Sixty Years of Light Work *Fred Bentham 450pp* **£26.95** ISBN: 9781904031079
This title is an autobiography of one of the great names behind the development of modern stage lighting equipment and techniques. It includes a complete facsimile of the famous Strand Electric Catalogue of May 1936 – a reference work in itself.

Sound for the Stage *Patrick Finelli 218pp* **£24.95** ISBN: 9781904031154
Patrick Finelli's thorough manual covering all aspects of live and recorded sound for performance is a complete training course for anyone interested in working in the field of stage sound, and is a must for any student of sound.

Stage Automation *Anton Woodward 128pp* **£12.95** ISBN: 9781904031567
The purpose of this book is to explain the stage automation techniques used in modern theatre to achieve some of the spectacular visual effects seen in recent years. The book is targeted at automation operators, production managers, theatre technicians, stage engineering machinery manufacturers and theatre engineering students. Topics are covered in sufficient detail to provide an insight into the thought processes that the stage automation engineer has to consider when designing a control system to control stage machinery in a modern theatre. The author has worked on many stage automation projects and developed the award-winning Impressario stage automation system.

Stage Lighting Design in Britain: The Emergence of the Lighting Designer, 1881-1950
Nigel Morgan 300pp **£17.95** ISBN: 9781904031345
This title sets out to ascertain the main course of events and the controlling factors that determined the emergence of the theatre lighting designer in Britain, starting with the introduction of incandescent electric light to the stage, and ending at the time of the first public lighting design credits around 1950. The book explores the practitioners, equipment, installations and techniques of lighting design.

Stage Lighting for Theatre Designers *Nigel Morgan 124pp* **£17.95**
ISBN: 9781904031192
This is an updated second edition of Nigel Morgan's popular book for students of theatre design – outlining all the techniques of stage lighting design.

Technical Marketing – Ideas for Engineers *David Brooks. 376pp* **£26.95**
ISBN: 9781904031857
When *Technical Marketing Techniques* was published in 2000, marketing was poised on the threshold of a new era. What advertising and design agencies then termed 'new media' was merely a glimpse of what was to follow as the Internet came to dominate and transform the way we did things. We coined the term Technical Marketing to describe a new way of operating for businesses and how they marketed their products and services on a global platform. 'Technical Marketing – Ideas for Engineers' retains a major opening section covering traditional marketing theory and then in the second section demonstrates how online and offline techniques can be integrated into an effective marketing communications plan. The final section of the book reviews the still evolving possibilities of digital marketing which is beginning to re write the rules of marketing.

Technical Standards for Places of Entertainment (2015) *ABTT 366pp A4* **£60.00**
ISBN: 9781904031833
Technical Standards for Places of Entertainment details the necessary physical standards required for entertainment venues. Known in the industry as the "Yellow Book" the latest completely revised edition was first published in June 2015.

Theatre Engineering and Stage Machinery *Toshiro Ogawa 344pp* **£30.00**
ISBN: 9781904031888
Theatre Engineering and Stage Machinery is a unique reference work covering every aspect of theatrical machinery and stage technology in global terms, and across the complete

historical spectrum. Revised April 2016 to include addendum on ideal layouts for opera houses.

Theatre Lighting in the Age of Gas   *Terence Rees   232pp*   **£24.95**
ISBN: 9781904031178
Entertainment Technology Press has republished this valuable historic work previously produced by the Society for Theatre Research in 1978. Theatre Lighting in the Age of Gas investigates the technological and artistic achievements of theatre lighting engineers from the 1700s to the late Victorian period.

Theatre Space: A Rediscovery Reported   *Francis Reid   238pp*   **£19.95**
ISBN: 9781904031437
In the post-war world of the 1950s and 60s, the format of theatre space became a matter for a debate that aroused passions of an intensity unknown before or since. The proscenium arch was clearly identified as the enemy, accused of forming a barrier to disrupt the relations between the actor and audience. An uneasy fellow-traveller at the time, Francis Reid later recorded his impressions whilst enjoying performances or working in theatres old and new and this book is an important collection of his writings in various theatrical journals from 1969-2001 including his contribution to the Cambridge Guide to the Theatre in 1988. It reports some of the flavour of the period when theatre architecture was rediscovering its past in a search to establish its future.

The Theatres and Concert Halls of Fellner and Helmer   *Michael Sell   246pp*   **£23.95**
ISBN: 9781904031772
This is the first British study of the works of the prolific Fellner and Helmer Atelier which was active from 1871-1914 during which time they produced over 80 theatre designs and are second in quantity only to Frank Matcham, to whom reference is made.
This period is one of great change as a number of serious theatre fires which included Nice and Vienna had the effect of the introduction of safety legislation which affected theatre design. This study seeks to show how Fellner and Helmer and Frank Matcham dealt with this increasing safety legislation, in particular the way in which safety was built into their new three part theatres equipped with iron stages, safety curtains, electricity and appropriate access and egress and, in the Vienna practice, how this was achieved across 13 countries.

Theatres of Achievement   *John Higgins   302pp*   **£29.95**   ISBN: 9781904031376
John Higgins affectionately describes the history of 40 distinguished UK theatres in a personal tribute, each uniquely illustrated by the author. Completing each profile is colour photography by Adrian Eggleston.

A Theatric Miscellany   *Francis Reid   154pp*   **£15.95**   ISBN: 9781904031871
This book is about memories. Some of them are highlights of the author's life. Recall of other, more routine events, is triggered by discovery of a cache of sundry articles. A few make predictions that are still relevant but most guess the future wrongly. Either way, they make a small contribution to history.

Theatric Tourist *Francis Reid 220pp* **£19.95** ISBN: 9781904031468
Theatric Tourist is the delightful story of Francis Reid's visits across more than 50 years to theatres, theatre museums, performances and even movie theme parks. In his inimitable style, the author involves the reader within a personal experience of venues from the Legacy of Rome to theatres of the Renaissance and Eighteenth Century Baroque and the Gustavian Theatres of Stockholm. His performance experiences include Wagner in Beyreuth, the Pleasures of Tivoli and Wayang in Singapore. This is a 'must have' title for those who are as "incurably stagestruck" as the author.

Through the Viewfinder *Jeremy Hoare 276pp* **£21.95** ISBN:: 9781904031574
Do you want to be a top television cameraman? Well this is going to help!
Through the Viewfinder is aimed at media students wanting to be top professional television cameramen – but it will also be of interest to anyone who wants to know what goes on behind the cameras that bring so much into our homes.
The author takes his own opinionated look at how to operate a television camera based on 23 years' experience looking through many viewfinders for a major ITV network company. Based on interviews with people he has worked with, all leaders in the profession, the book is based on their views and opinions and is a highly revealing portrait of what happens behind the scenes in television production from a cameraman's point of view.

Vectorworks for Theatre *Steve Macluskie 232pp* **£23.95** ISBN: 9781904031826
An essential reference manual for anyone using Vectorworks in the Theatre Industry. This book covers everything from introducing the basic tools to creating 3D design concepts and using worksheets to calculate stock usage and lighting design paperwork. A highly visual style using hundreds of high resolution screen images makes this a very easy book to follow whether novice or experienced user.

Walt Disney Concert Hall – The Backstage Story *Patricia MacKay & Richard Pilbrow 250pp* **£28.95** ISBN: 9781904031239
Spanning the 16-year history of the design and construction of the Walt Disney Concert Hall, this book provides a fresh and detailed behind the scenes story of the design and technology from a variety of viewpoints. This is the first book to reveal the "process" of the design of a concert hall.

West End in Watercolour – A Portrait of London Theatre *John Higgins 260pp* **£28.95** ISBN: 9781904031925
Today London is widely regarded as the theatrical epicentre of the English-speaking world, its 'West End' closely rivalled by New York's Broadway, and provides a rich array of theatres, opera houses, concert halls and cinemas which, alongside the delights of restaurants, cafes, pubs, bars, nightclubs and shops, create a glitteringly exciting playground for the would-be theatregoer.
While John Higgins considers the West End and its fashionable rise from earlier beginnings, he also looks closely at the concurrent vigorous entertainment scene around the East End and neighbouring working-class suburbs, and their subsequent metamorphosis into the prolific operation that has today become the trendy Off-West-End London Fringe.

And so as the typical famous grand 'Up West' houses are paraded in their glittering surroundings of glamour and razzamatazz, their fascinating 'Off-West' counterparts have their own exciting tales to tell ... and John says one thing is for sure: they have all been delicious to paint!

Yesterday's Lights – A Revolution Reported *Francis Reid 352pp* **£26.95**
ISBN: 9781904031321
Set to help new generations to be aware of where the art and science of theatre lighting is coming from – and stimulate a nostalgia trip for those who lived through the period, Francis Reid's latest book has over 350 pages dedicated to the task, covering the 'revolution' from the fifties through to the present day. Although this is a highly personal account of the development of lighting design and technology and he admits that there are 'gaps', you'd be hard put to find anything of significance missing.

Go to www.etbooks.co.uk for full details of above titles and secure online ordering facilities. Most books also available for Kindle.